PRAISE FOR *Winners Have Yet to Be An*

"Ed Pavlić shapes the ineffable (some cal
into a language haunting the borders of the ~~~~~~~~~~~~~~~~~~~
the sung and unsung. He casts Hathaway as Orpheus searching 'for
an opening between need and can't have and have and can't need.'
Winners Have Yet to Be Announced is a meditation on our own
between-ness: our wish to be rooted pulling against our wish to
transcend. It is a visionary book."
— TERRANCE HAYES, author of *Wind in a Box*

"Pavlić's wide-ranging, lyrical approach matches Hathaway's virtuosity
and honors him with equal amounts of soul and heart. He seems
nourished by the innards of Hathaway's life, both intellectual and
spiritual—and how can he not but be inspired? *Winners Have Yet
to Be Announced* is a hammered book about the tragic eloquence of
a man's life."
— MAJOR JACKSON, author of *Hoops*

"Ed Pavlić's tribute to Donny Hathaway is stunning. Pavlić writes the
way Hathaway sang. Can you hear it? Terror and joy ride the wave
together. This is a song, sung over a song, sung over another song and
another, until it finds expression through a strange angel of a human."
— JOY HARJO, author of *How We Became Human*

"Donny Hathaway traced the lonely line between gospel and the blues
and tried to tell us that 'Someday We'll All Be Free,' though in the
end he was perhaps unable to believe it himself. Pavlić's compelling
meditation on Hathaway allows us to see how grace can grow in the
cracks of city sidewalks and redemption may catch us even when we
leap from its grasp."
— TIMOTHY B. TYSON, author of *Blood Done Sign My Name*

"A dearth of original interview material has led to much speculation about the creative process, inner workings, and mental turmoil that made the late Donny Hathaway a black icon beyond his thirty-three years. Using the art of vivid poetic prose and imagery, Pavlić paints a portrait of a brilliant artist possessed by music, a nonetheless reluctant live performer whose ability to evoke emotion and provoke response among his audience transcended his own often deeply troubled state of mind. Through Pavlić's work, we are left with a greater understanding and comprehension of Hathaway, both man and musical master."

— DAVID NATHAN, author of *The Soulful Divas*

"*Winners Have Yet to Be Announced* is my book of the year. In jazzy and poetic prose, Hathaway and his imaginary biographer carry us across space and time. We walk through the near physical landscape of Hathaway's aesthetic mind as they talk — in voices at once pungent and real, poetic and philosphical."

— BINYAVANGA WAINAINA, editor of *Kwani?*

"Since Miles all music has been made with excerptable bits — nuggets for DJs to feast on, quotable breaks for the damaged. All that delicious shit that kept Madiba's spirit intact — do you know his favorite question to the world is 'What's going on?' Pavlić warns: Hold up with the premature autopsies, *Winners Have Yet to Be Announced*. He warns: The flat line is not anaesthetic, there's beauty in it — listen to dead cellphone batteries. He asks that we listen, that we turn the volume down."

— NTONE EDJABE, editor of *Chimurenga*

Winners Have Yet to Be Announced

WINNERS HAVE YET TO BE ANNOUNCED

A Song for Donny Hathaway

POEMS BY ED PAVLIĆ

THE UNIVERSITY OF GEORGIA PRESS

Athens & London

Published by The University of Georgia Press

Athens, Georgia 30602

© 2008 by Ed Pavlić

All rights reserved

Designed by Walton Harris

Set in 10.5/15 Garamond Premier

Printed and bound by Thomson-Shore

The paper in this book meets the guidelines for permanence
and durability of the Committee on Production Guidelines
for Book Longevity of the Council on Library Resources.

Printed in the United States of America

12 11 10 09 08 P 5 4 3 2 1

Library of Congress Control Number: 2007941566

ISBN-13: 978-0-8203-3097-6

ISBN-10: 0-8203-3097-3

British Library Cataloging-in-Publication Data available

for Ric

He would be like a movie director. He would direct himself saying, "I have to be more in love here."

— ARIF MARDIN

Contents

Winners Have Yet to Be Announced

I

I love music, period.

— DONNY HATHAWAY

Interview : Cause of Death :
A Sound or Something Like It :

February 15, 1979 : Chicago, IL

Sure, you could say I knew it, we all knew it all along. Or did we?
It hit me somehow, different, when they showed me the report :
"multiple fractures and internal injuries."

I mean we all knew how he died. Didn't we? So, why so different
when I actually saw the report? There it was, things spun into focus.
It was like when you stare out a train window at trees blurring by and
suddenly turn your head against the motion of the train. The blur
stops and, for an instant, there's one tree standing before your eyes.
Or falling.

He'd been there for years. Trying on disciplines. Midair right there in front of us. Propped himself upright and forced himself to look the other way. Shem in the funny-house mirror. Running scared. Once in a while, a quick glimpse off stage. Fresh out from two and a half hours in the shower. Head out the window, fingers of steam from his uncombed hair. Or now and again, say up in his place on La Salle, a look on his face'd hit you like a brick thrown across the room. Tenth floor. A chipped brick suspended in a bright angle-beam of low, winter light, halfway out the kitchen window with a wooden spoon, singing, "Hold me down . . . you can't hold me down . . ." to the snow and the pigeons and to the dude he said was always waiting for him. Mr. Soul he called him. Waiting for him, to bump shoulders with him, down in the street. Falling backward in from the ledge. Laughing and singing, "Only way to enter a room full of friends, fall in backward thru the window." Cold falling over the windowsill, spilling over him on the floor. Tears running down, filling his ears.

Already too late. Already by then, people would talk to him and he just wouldn't respond. Soon, frustrated, or in disbelief, they'd usually leave quietly. I remember once, after some reviewer had left, he turned to me and said, "It took years before I could tell if someone's talking to me. And, more than that, that most people never say word the first. Years. And, after I knew it, it's a crime how long it took me to believe it was actually possible. More years. Right there, sitting across from me, they look in my eyes and wipe me clean off the slate. Like, what street do you live on . . . me? I'm up on Tabula Rasa. I didn't want to believe it. Right there, right here, and nowhere. Welcome to the clean slate. You want to know why *he* ain't heavy?"

Said, "They say Einstein died padding around his attic in Princeton looking for a Unified Theory . . . I went to hear Baldwin talk to kids at a junior high school in Harlem. He said, 'We have a problem, the problem is at once simple and very complicated. It's that many people by now have realized that it's no longer fashionable to be a racist. Fewer, however, have come to account for how very difficult it is to be, you know, a *person*.' At the time, I didn't know what he was talking about, still don't. But, I think I know by now something about the empty feeling that made him say it like that, up there in front of those kids and their teachers. Because he knew he didn't know, exactly, either. He said it just like that, man, then he stood there quiet, slightly queenish and ironic in his lime green foulard; he took all the eyes on him and just stood there with his hands on the sides of the podium, jaw moving around lightly like he was rolling a mouthful of red wine in the back of his mouth, like he was chewing on the back part of his tongue."

v

Maybe the tabula rasa trip wouldn't have been so bad if people didn't come wanting to talk about music. He said, "It was the relief. Not emotional relief. It was something in the topography of their faces. The different planes, the tension between the molten face and the map of the solid one people try to hand off in conversations." I can hear him now, "look, is this a conversation or a bedtime story?" Said he could see it as it happened, word by word, whole sentences went opaque. Off limits. Said he could see the language laid out like a map of the sea floor : troughs and ridges, trenches and ripples of sand like the ones on the roof of your mouth. Middle of someone's question, I'd see him turn inward as if to see if he couldn't quick turn the blank phrase around before it'd be too late. He'd take his finger and trace designs in the table top, compulsive sketches, webs over an empty manhole. Irreversible if it takes.

Whole sections of the spoken language on the scrap heap. Worse than silence. A kind of sound with no song, with no roots in silence. He'd begun to call the shit people hand each other "death sentences." I can hear him now, "counterfeit flesh-bridges, webs of agreed-upon delusions." He'd say, "Before long, that's all we'll have left, in every language, 'fainting in tongues' and 'death sentences.' Both dumbstruck in their own ways and completely numb to the subtle rhythms that connect thought to what's beneath it." He'd turn from a conversation, "Hear that? Say that shit in the dark three times and see if it don't make you want to spit like if you think about sucking on a slice of lemon. Words inside words. They leave you craving salt. Paper dolls." He'd turn, "how I'm going to look, a grown man, talking to paper dolls?"

Once, I said, "Sure but look, people have to have something to say.
Something to talk about. Otherwise, they'd just go crazy. Listen to the
incessant chatter. Waves of it. Fear. What other explanation is there?"

And he : "It used to be enough for me to say that. It's not enough,
now. My mother did other people's laundry to survive. She didn't. So
now what? *I'm* ... me? *I'm* supposed to do other people's wash so *they*
can live dead and call it a pleasant evening? Not hardly. The truth is
they wouldn't *go* crazy if they quit the chatter. They ARE crazy, man.
It's already happened. And, that's fine. I've known crazy people all my
life. There are some who can just be quiet, don't have to slobber on
you all day long. I've known people, some crazy some not, who could
fill a room with beautiful light just with their own kind of silence. But,
these folks, they come to me for a cure.

Then they don't want to be cured. Entertained. I say, 'If it's a full
house, deuces and jacks, then it's a full house deuces and jacks. Lay
them down. But, you know, don't come around telling me your trio
of jacks are *all* spades!' I say, 'If you want this healed, it's got to be
re-broke.' It's a lot to ask of music, then, isn't it? To be song and silence
at the same time to people hell-bent on holding them in separate,
what do they call them, neutral corners? To be a conversation that
everyone needs but no one's going near. That's what it gets down
to, man, clear away the bullshit, create shade, some quiet space, and
sweep it away before anyone notices. It was there. And, you know
these crowds. They don't even give you a chance. They don't trust
themselves alone in the dark.

I sing, 'Our time's short and precious.' I sing, 'You don't have to
wear false charms.' Crowds act like they only hear the damn chorus.
I suppose it sounds ok in a crowd, if you're part of a crowd. "Be
Real Black for Me?" I know, I know, but come *on*. What is a crowd,
anyway? A benign mob? A mob in waiting? In wanting? But, that's
why it sells, right? And, crowds can be beautiful. Trouble with them
is that they can't go home. 'Ok, it's a bit obsessive.' He'd sing it with
cloudy, falsetto eyes. 'Obses-sive.' But, more and more, for me . . .
I can't . . . Look, a part of a crowd has no home, man. On the other
hand, what part of the song holds up, like with a painting, alone in
a room? The streets seem somehow full of guerilla sentinels at ready
to assassinate the answer to that question, to kill any pause, poised to
blurt out something, some-fool anything, into any window I leave
open. Truth is there isn't an open window in this goddamned town.
Truth is, there just isn't *that* much to say." And, his brow curled up for
an instant and I heard his voice shake, "but there's *so* much to hear!
And, outside the crowd, almost nothing to sell . . . No one wants to
feel the breeze, no one wants to talk about that —

One night, walking just off Cottage Grove, we turned into a
storefront service and I felt him blast off in his seat. Real rage
and despair. Afterwards, inconsolable, he said he could tell from the
sermon which song'd be next. Said, "Man, I guessed three in a
row! And just as bad, they still use minor downstairs and major for
tears on the way up. . . ." You know how, if someone's really terrified,
their voice sort of gurgles somewhere, underneath, like they're
drowning somewhere under themselves? That night he learned to
play *that* sound with his left hand . . . learned it right then and there.
I watched. One minute he didn't have it, never asked. The next, there
it is in his left hand. And I remember that beam of light on chipped
brick thing happening again in his face. He said, "Well, there's
something . . . ." After that, he'd sing you a song and drown it with
his left hand . . . he said, "If I can predict where he's going, why the
hell should I pretend?" We got up and left out the church.

Down the street, and he : "How many times do you have to count change in an empty pocket? He knows what they want and so do they. Minor, bad. Major, good. Q and A. Leading the witness. But, that little girl, third from the left, *she* wasn't singing it that way." And me : I couldn't hear her. And he : "Me either, couldn't barely hear anyone with that possessed boy on the drums . . . didn't need to hear her, I could tell by one look at her face . . . don't know where she's headed, but, I'll tell you *this*, she's not long for *that* church! You don't need faith for that kind of hand-slap noise. But, that thing you need that you don't have and you don't need it yet. *Need*. Should have to have a permit just to use the word. And things you need, you only need them once, man. And the question isn't how *much* do you need . . . that's x and y axis stuff. The question is *how* do you need? Just how? Need happens once because it's not an amount. Not some kind of fool's choice between less and fewer. Should and shouldn't need not apply. Down there where the only thing that's certain is that nothing's arbitrary. Need's an infinite array of qualities. *That's* the beauty. That's the difficulty. They only come together like they do once. Next time, the quality is different. So, need and faith are the same things. They're echoes of each other. Faith is a singular event. And so the question. Will it be there when you need it? No one knows *that* answer. That's why it's faith. The infinite qualities of need and the singular reality of faith." I said, 'Identical twins.' And he, "Identical? Shit, they're Chang and Eng. Sing *that*?! Otherwise, anyway you go, you end up looking for music in a cabbage patch, songs hanging from bandanas in a stork's beak."

We found a lounge with a piano, terrible old dusty thing. Ordered
two drinks. Downed his, "I needed that." Laughter. He sat down and
started to moan his way, picking thru those speeches, those sermons
under his breath. Sang, "want to know what faith's for . . . no, you
don't want to know what faith is for, maybe baby needs some more,
maybe for the one waiting, for you, for *you*, outside *every* door . . ."
I used to love to watch him play in public, unannounced. It's not like
the records, not even the live ones . . . especially not the live ones.
Because it wasn't really public and it wasn't hardly private. I know he
scared people, man. I'm not talking about audiences who spent hours
getting ready for him. Posters and haircuts, costumes and painted
nails . . . he used to say, "Wonder when they'll just break out the suits
of armor?" Forget about that. When he played these incognito nights,
it was like catching a glimpse of yourself in an unexpected mirror. You
say, "Who's that?" and realize you haven't seen yourself in months,
maybe years. I remember how he'd rage : "You want to talk about
Orlando Furioso, Angelica's ring? It's a bitch, ain't it? About the only
people ever heard *me* play are those who never knew it was *me*. All I
have to do is take off this hat . . . I'm invisible."

moan it under the breath and a right hand moves like an echo of water under water

"You know an echo comes back in reverse right?" Left hand
spilling over his face like hot water gushing into a porcelain tub.
"You know the second rainbow's a reflection of the first?" Said,
"We have so much to do and undo, I'm talking about history, man."
Said, "Monteverdi invented the tremolo staring over a canal at
sundown in Venice. He used it every night to make the rich folks
cry. Want a history of modern music? Start with Monteverdi's letter
to Striggio, 9 December, 1616 : it's a critique of what a poor use of
language does to music. Cut through all the 'His Serene Highness'
and 'if you bid me speak' noise and you know what's left? Failure.
And the clash of material interests : wealth and truth. Oresme hadn't
made it out of the scholastic shadows and Opera hadn't made it to
Venice and, hell, it was still a generation or two before Descartes's
Meditations on First Philosophy."

And me : Hello? Earth to Donny in the way-back machine . . .

Hello? *So*, the market, *Venice*, hadn't penetrated the aesthetic and
before rationalism and the clean slate had taken out tooth and root,
an artist could still hold his head up and consider truth a material
interest. *That's* hello in the way-back. All you had to do was slip it
by the pope, and, let's face it, that had to be about as hard as getting
rid of free gas in LA these days. And remember, it was still such an
interesting braid of East and West that it doesn't make sense, really,
even to use the words. The Vatican still treasured references to the
Holy Land in Arabic. Rich folks in Venice draped Muslim prayer
rugs across their shoulders for portraits. In *Madonna and Child*,
Giotto wrapped the Madonna in tiraz, cuffs embroidered with chants
to honor past Muslim rulers. Granted that was the 14th century,
but Fabriano, Maestro Andreoli sustained the practice into the late
16th century. Look, even after 1600, in Florence, the Medici Factory
had a method of imitating the Chinese secret for true porcelain and
decorated vases with imitation Turkish floral patterns. The rhythm
of blood in braided veins. They *should* have been imitating the Turks!
The Turks *made* the Medici! Well, the Turks and Pius II with his alum
monopoly. But you know about that —

And me : Ah . . .

Alum, this was what they call a mordant. A treatment that allowed colors to adhere to fabrics and other surfaces . . . The Turks had taken over most of the European mines for alum, the most important mordant of the time. They imposed huge tribute payments that made the price for the possibility of color quintuple in Europe. Then, they discovered huge alum deposits in Tolfa, in the pope's territory. Long story short, the pope got rich selling his alum to the courts of Europe (after he'd forbidden doing business with the godless Turks, of course).

Ok, but you said it made the Medici rich?

They were the bank. They beat out the Genoese bankers for the rights to middle man the Pope's monopoly on color. Of course, the proceeds from the sale filtered back to the Pope who used the money to finance the crusades, they called it 'crusade alum,' against the Turks. Doubtless, the Medici could see that getting rich and financing a war against the source of the income was bizarre behavior, but, they rode it out anyway.

A little review?

Ok. If there's no "West" in the Renaissance that created the West? You know there's no virgin birth. Else, why aren't we all walking on water by now? I love that. The Turks created the channels that created the Renaissance by holding the possibility of color hostage. The pope and the bankers took advantage of the hostage. Nothing changes, does it? That is to say, nothing stays itself for very long.

I think the review needs review, D.

And the left hand started boiling down chords with that underwater gurgle-moan. His right hand punctuating certain words with thirds, flatted fifths. "The point is the loom of history. Woven and dyed and stolen and entangled and untangled. Bought, sold, stolen, and resold. If we'd actually look at the nubile routes humans invented to move them through their own histories, we'd be somewhere else right now. Which is the catch, the key insight. We *are* somewhere else, right now! Maybe close by. So, you know, why not be *there*? Why sit in the empty chair next to yourself? Forget the big war banners and all the goose step heresies to the human spirit that litter our brains . . . When we think of the past beneath the present, and I mean *just* beneath, and I mean the *human* present, forget: 'Dick and Jane Climb from the Fallout Shelter for an Afternoon in Disneyland.' Instead of waiting for noses to fall off — or plotting to *blow* them off — monuments in marble, we need to imagine underground rivers, rainwater purified as it seeps thru layers of rock and dirt. That's all day everyday. That's where we come from all day everyday. Humanity's history isn't a black robed court case of headlines, man. See that coming, think : tar baby. Think, 'Walk on By . . .' Right hand chords, 'Walk on By-y-y.' For the living truth of the species, think : the glow of lightning in a thunder cloud cut out by the project rooftops; the reflection of the storm in four rain-puddles the shape of footprints that face each other, toe to toe, in the tar on the roof; the rhythm of a worm's pulse under the broken pavement; the play of light and death behind your closed lids; this low-moan left hand in for what you can't hear in the distance, in for the dark blue curl and white foam of your brain at the beach. This is who we are. *That's* a person."

Look, so, how'd Monteverdi put it : 'either the delicate, instruments
that is, will be improper or the proper ones not delicate.' It has to be
that way, *we* untie the knots. The knots are us. Each other. So, back to
the assignment : history of music :

50 ways to lie about faith and figure a new way to make rich folks cry.
And still, as Monteverdi put it to Striggio, as you say, in 'the way back,'
'attend to the singing speech; and not, as here, to spoken song.' And
there we're getting to it. And we're not even going to talk about the
missing link : like how there's no peaceful way to get from hydrogen
and helium to the heavier elements. Say, for instance, rubbing his arm,
again, "Carbon. Fifteen million degrees, man. Can you say boom!"
Pedal down, it sounds like he fell on the keys like falling down a flight
of steps. "The ever-living flesh and its real, material mysteries. But,
that's just the artist's dilemma, we haven't really touched on language,
music and the ill-uses of the listener?" He turns to face the people in
the booths, "Anyone in here feel like talking about the ill-uses of the
listeners? About what people hear, what they won't hear and a little
something about why?" No pause. "Thought not." His laugh. "About
who pays what for hearing, and about who pays how much to cover
their . . . you know I almost said ears?" Then, "speaking of open circles,
how about another drink?"

After a while, people in the place'd go back to their conversations and he'd keep playing. Then he'd drown that song in a sound I haven't heard since and most of those people never heard at all.

Middle of a song, he'd ask, "You think we're talking right now?"

And me : "You tell me . . ."

His laugh. If that's what you'd call it. I could hear him modulate his laughter. High tenor. Scary. He'd pound a chord, hold the pedal, press his left hand into that big, meaty thigh and act like he's really letting loose. All the time his eyes *on* you like they're staring through barbed wire. A smile inverted, augmented, seventh slid up and diminished. You can see it now if you want to, see if I'm lying. Take a good look, hell, take half a one-eyed look, at the cover of *Everything Is Everything*. You call *that* a smile? Just another go-lucky day with the kids, right? Right. Happy day in the new Black nation, right? Morning in the homeland of the soul. Right? Show him what he's won, Bob.

And he : "And, I want to talk, man, bad. Hand over all my records for one conversation. Hand over all my — well, *half* my money . . . Serious. Simple things. Sit and talk and be there, man. Hold hands and talk. *Talk*, hear me, let the roof come in. Hand over a shoulder. Let the fucking doors freeze shut. With anyone. What? It's supposed to matter? After everything? How? But, not this incessant half-assed chat. Not this rubber mallet and garden hose filled with sand shit. He blows and blows and blows leave no bruise. Isn't that a technique for torture? And what next, enlightenment? The silent drip of clear water into a bowl? Talk. And not rushed like this and not the contest, the soulless and meaningless joust for answers. Not Socrates and the yes men. Not this, 'we can talk if you can get these three questions right.' Not this preacher wearing waders in the water, hot feet on thin ice stuff.

Not that, because, afterward, it gets, it's like I can't any longer stand it, afterward. *Petit mort*. What happens. Waves of it like wild surf coming at you. But, it doesn't get closer. Not at you. The waves back up off the shore. Wild surf coming *from* you. Same voices sound different. Like if you spin a record backward and the men sound like women and the women turn into strings. Strings into wind, wind to ice and breath to bent steel and so on. So, it's a kind of discipline I've tried, you know, in desperation really, to create. I *have* tried. Life and times of an unplayed card, man. Then I can hear something, it's something like hearing, and I can imagine sitting and talking to a person. A sound like a conversation between face-down cards. Waves crash in the far distance. There's a sound. Truth is, though, the sound's only there because you know it's there. Where does that leave us? 'The Mood,' a duet, a conversation with no words." His hands hover over the keys like eye-level hawks just off the ridge. Vultures off Muir Point. "After a while, she got tired of it, seems to me like she just got tired of it. Played her hand and raked in her chips. And, then there's me, and one day, I know Mr. Soul downstairs will follow me up to the room, whatever room I'm in by then . . . and he's not going to want to *talk*, I'll tell you that.

"You know, in the old movies, remember how the submarine captains hid out on the ocean floor. Undershirts . . . you know, everyone sweats. The enemy above. They called it 'radio silence,' right? They sit there and wait and watch each other breathe and then they get away. Isn't that great? That's just *like* us, now."

And me : "But, away to where, D? You going to live in the veins under the earth?"

And he : "Deep! The Red Sea, man. It wasn't dry, it was deep. People shouting about 'Get Down, Moses! . . .' Maybe they're right after all." His laugh. And the barbed wire. "Remember the folks in Hyde Park Cinema yelling at Mr. Heston, 'Don't forget the snorkel, Moses!' An opening, a passage. Maybe the way out was quiet. A sound or something like it. Patterned silence. Like in the silent way your body learns a song. A sound that left no story behind and it crossed between lovers in their sleep. Waves in a distant nearing you couldn't see, or hear, a distance that washes over you like from out of nowhere. Improvisation all in the milky innards. That's the man-*and*-the-damned-date. What'd that poet write about love and the 'rigorous laws of risk'? About : 'does not pamper, will not spare'?

Take me and you. The Black nation. Take any two of these good
people." He waves his arm. An ice cube twirls and, achieving escape
velocity, arcs across thru the room toward a couple in a booth. The
cube travels along the floor to stop, apparently unnoticed, beneath
the leather-loafer-soled apex in the toe-tap of a man's foot as he listens
to his woman's story. His face a portrait of calm agreement. A quick,
quarter-rest for two double takes, a wry smile and, then, in a whisper,
"Is it fashion? I hear talk like we could buy our own skin and send it
into battle against ourselves. I'm all for Lorraine and Nina, man, but,
what? I'm supposed to sing all about gifts for the young while nobody
seems to listen, gone to tongues by then, at how the song ends. Or,
really, how it doesn't end. Never ends. Like there's one road, a cul-de-
sac and a hairstyle has a mind of its own? As if it could walk around
without us. People. I think about Modigliani, an early piece, a little
piece of somber Tuscany. Before Paris. He painted the empty road out
of Tuscany, 14-years-old, painted it in bed getting over typhoid. Then
he went the opposite way. For the rest of his short life, he painted
people he loved. I think about Baldwin, that fluent angle in his neck,
chewing on his tongue. He was holding a window open. As if to say,
'look at that old man over there smoking his drink. Which one is he,
young or gifted? Is his song over or not begun? Is he a person or an
option? I'll tell you what, if *he*'s an option, you don't have a damned
nation.' All that and he never said a word to explain, all that from
rolling wine in an empty mouth.

Sometimes I feel like the only places we share are the ones no one's ever been to. I mean, Jesus, that's terrible. 'Be Real Black for Me?' I know, I know, monuments with no noses. But, tell me, what the hell does a friend need with a body that's 'strong and stately'? Stately? Good Lord, shake your head free of the crowd and listen to that verse three times in light of the dark. Which phrases make it? Make sense." He pauses, holds up his right arm and rubs his skin, "sense, makes sense . . . you know, the material mystery. Try it. The only phrase that rings true is 'you don't have . . .' Here it is again, tell me I'm wrong." He plays the chord :

"*You* don't have, to wear false charms."

That turned a few heads. I heard someone say, "who *is* that?" Someone else, "is he somebody?" After a moment, the murmurs of the conversations grew like cotton in the ears and filled in the space. And he : "It's plainly there in the tone, an anonymous confession in the tone, ' . . . to wear false charms' is window dressing . . . narrative. End of the day, it's 'you don't have.' There it is. Beautiful all by itself. An empty Tuscan road. Can you hear in the dark? Yes, you can. God bless the child that knows what he *don't have*, who knows what he's missing . . . what he, a person, *needs*. I mean to be a person.

XXV

And me : So, this is about missing persons and empty roads.

'Hey, someone score one for the mystery guest. You got it, "Livorno," 1898, Oil on cardboard. Look, just for a moment, ok, let's forget all the other stuff about, you know, 'wake up every morning and pull a rabbit from out the hat.' It can't go home. If it can't go home, it's a lying in the street. For me, it's got to work *back*stage. Alone in the dark. Then, of course, there's *home*.

Home?

He hit the chord again, "We were alone . . . we-e were alone . . . and I was playing this song . . ." He moaned the rest. I heard someone say, "I know who *that* is . . ." And, he smiled to one side of his mouth and tipped the side of his head in the direction of the voice.

"They'll say there's more to it than that, than this." He plays the chord again, holds it til it fades. And, then plays it again, "There is more to it than that. They're right. So, why the act, you know, as if there's so damned much *less* to it than us? I want to talk about people. Forget music. I want to talk about sweeping up broken glass. About who threw the bottle. The thrower, the throw, the *loving* feeling and the thrown. About the real, new, the *lost* and the shattered, whole thing."

And me : But what's there to say about that?

"Now, there, you see?" Another chord, broken, with his right hand, "You *do* get my point . . . now let's get before they figure out I really am who I'm not supposed to be." And the left hand washes in like steam from behind the pseudo-Turkish flowers painted on the imitation Chinese porcelain of his eyes. Eyes that said nothing if they didn't say what it meant to be wide open.

II

In the studio he'd been talking to us in one voice and then answering himself in another. Other times he'd sit down at the piano and play all these fantastic classical themes, stuff he'd written himself. We cut what we could during lucid periods. In the end, the nurse he had with him didn't ultimately save his life. My view is he should have never been left on his own.

— ERIC MERCURY

Listening Notes : Mercy Medical Psychiatric :

January 13, 1973 : Chicago, IL

Most of them play it way too loud. Maybe they've already sold their souls to noise. Make noise out of anything. Fill mountain air with car horns. Up early, jack hammers with toothbrush fittings. Up late, I've seen them hang chimes off sills to keep the wind from sneaking thru the bars on their bedroom windows. Up all night.

Maybe life itself has become a kind of manic noise? Even the quiet's made of noise. White noise. Planned activities. Conversations morphed into guided tours. People keep their brains ready for visitors. Visiting hours. More like open houses than conversations. Want to know where I was a year ago last Tuesday, 2–3:30. I'll get my planner . . . Yep. Like I thought, here it is, 2–3:30, nowhere, talking with no one.

ii

Me too, I sing them too loud. But, in my head, they're somewhere
beneath whispers. Volume, yes, immense volume, but not loud. Or
quiet. It really has nothing to do with amps. Amplitude silent as karst
in the fog on rice paper. Majestic, even, the longevity of a wave has its
own sounds.

You mean wave length?
You again? Can't you wait outside in the street anymore?
It's raining.
How'd you get in?
Don't worry about that, you were saying?
Since you're so interested, no. I mean

volume. The way a song fills a room. Rooms after rooms. Like real
human flesh. Maybe you've heard of it? The way songs build, cloud my
head and spill down my arms. Just like with people, as if they've taught
my hands things and left me out of it. The way you learn to play music
from the inside out. You don't get to know a song by introducing
yourself. You can't just walk up on it like this here . . . There's no
guided tour. It won't shake your hand. You have to find an opening.

In the song?

Man, in yourself.

v

And, then, what of the other direction? Where you're taken, undeniably, out. Or up. The brain reels thru what it knows and comes up empty. Again and again. No frame for the place it's put you. High pressure : open your mouth and there's no worry about what might rush in. Open your mouth any old way up there and everything you have flies out. High enough, it can get absolutely physical.

*nude   he's on fire   he climbs over the rocks on the breakwater and
opens the blue with his body*

In electrocutions the lungs can come straight up and out of the
mouth. Like Donny B, the other Donny, of course, this is back when
I was the other Donny, when we were all just kids in Carr Square.
"St. Louis Blues." He'd climbed the telephone pole to pronounce a
toast to my birthday when that beer can hit the insulator. What then?
A flash like red and blue lightning and he's on his back in the street.
A half-swallowed octopus. Who are you going to be then? Victor
kneeling over him, clearing his mouth for his make-up-your-F-in-
summer-school's worth of CPR and wiping his hand on his jeans.
Victor pulling Donny B's lungs out of his mouth and wiping them on
his jeans. High pressure. That sound echoing down the street. That
sound and my wide open mouth. Then you're us, backing up down the
wet street, streaks of lung on Victor's jeans, and smoke coming out of
that boy's mouth. *Height.* After that, you can bet, part of you is always
backing up down the wet street . . .

Ok, height. But what if you're playing it?

You've disappeared.

No amount of clapping and shouting can bring you back. Ever. No lie smart enough to conjure your flesh back inside the skin. Can't be done anymore than we could have stuffed Victor's jeans back down D's smoking chest. Bone back into bone. Pressure. It's already happened. So, turn the volume down.

It's a little mystic, isn't it?

Man, one with the spirit? Not hardly. It's gothic. A medieval cathedral lit by torches. Those soaring stones, high arches. Ever hear music in one of those? Think of it back then without modern lights. Smell it. Remember, for heat, most people slept with their sheep and goats in the towering shadow. There's the sound. The height. Inside. The gothic arch, they brought height inside. The ceiling obscured by shadow and smoke. And the songs, polyphony shoots along the stones and up out of sight. Cause that's just about it, isn't it? Maybe it's more like the volume of sights than sounds? People go blind from pressure in their eyes.

Spheres aren't always enough. You know? The world as we find it?
Not enough, sometimes we need better than optimal. Three
dimensions worth of perfect won't get it. Volume over space. Any
ratio greater than one : depth. Less than one : height. Stay too far from
one, for too long and it's lights out, either way. Heraclitus sings blues
for Pythagoras.

The pressure of heights. It won't come in from out there. Forget out
there. If you're high, it's already inside and if it's inside it's on the
loose, searching for a way out. Depth, the constant sensation of being
surrounded. Suspended in sound. Depth : fear of invasion. Height :
of spontaneous effusion.

Seems easy to talk about it. But, you're never really talking about it.
Webs of refraction and inversion. Takes a *song*, a sound that can do
more than one thing at a time. It's the danger of singing. That's what
a song is. Got to where, if I even got close to a piano . . . I remember
when I was little, every piano I saw sounded to me like broken voices.
I couldn't play, really, but I could sit down and I'd just know how to
fix the voices. I got good at fixing voices, until, I began to hear things
behind the voices. Later, man, if I was anywhere near a piano, got to
where it felt just like sitting next to a roaring river. Spring run off.
That weight and speed and thunder. Problem was it felt like I couldn't
really find it. I could hear it, but, couldn't find where it'd come from.
And it seemed then that I'd have to swim the roar before I could
hear, let alone fix, the voices again. There are the keys, but, I'm lost in
the sound. Like I can hear it in the distance and at the same time it's
running right thru me but I can't find it. Soaking wet, dying of thirst.
Lost in and locked out of it? High, a song lost in the distance. Or,
or. Ice. Like I'd slipped, lost traction. To where I could feel myself
skating. Like I was dying of weightlessness, could feel gravity, a pull.
But, into what?

Afraid of the falls?

I was afraid, man. Damn straight. But, not of falling. Or swimming or
drowning. Not even of being lost.

None of the metaphors scared me. It was that none of the songs I
knew interested me. It was the crushing sense of all of it happening at
once. Everywhere. To everyone. And the sense of people so obviously
steeled against noticing. Afraid of what might happen. And the kicker
: it's already happened. August 18, 1950, in his diary, this is toward
the end, shit this *is* the end : Pavese wrote : 'The thing most feared in
secret always happens.' I don't think so. No, has *already* happened.
He thought it was a fear of depths. But it wasn't depth, the fear, it was
heights. That's the fear. It's in there already. That's the height. No. If
it hadn't already happened, the romantics would be enough. They'd
be perfect but for the *height*. But, for what's already happened, what's
already in there —

So, you see, it's not that people don't like good music. It's that they're afraid of heights. Ears pop. Mouths clenched. Look around you, see if people aren't holding themselves tight, like they're afraid of what they might do. Like they're standing on a cliff. That draw from over the edge . . . Like they're afraid to move. Look. Afraid of what might fly out under pressure . . . Their mouths don't even look like mouths, really, afraid of what they might say. Mouths look more like padlocks than mouths. Eyes behind the bars. And Depth. Others won't stop moving, couldn't stand still for a minute. Like a building that has to sway to stand. Depth, been down too long for down to bother me — Next verse should say 'someone stop me before I say the next thing and scare the life out of myself . . . someone teach me how to stop. And how to fall.' Depth. Want to know why you feel surrounded? Because you're surrounded.

Like I say, on some level, people must know this stuff. In the ward,
I used to see a man who'd walk the halls all day long. Strangest gait
you've ever seen. A shuffle. Right foot in back, left out front. Picture
him : right perpendicular to the line of motion, left in the line of
motion. He'd lean on his back right foot and gradually shift his
weight to his left in front. As he shifted his weight he'd gradually
move the back foot up to the front. Upside down capital T position.
Then, shifting back to the back foot, he'd slide the left foot forward.
Strangest thing. Repeated, absolutely without variation that I could
see. Miles like that. Deliberate. All day. Serious. All the while there
was any forward motion, always with the same foot, all his weight
was anchored to the back foot, straddling the path. And, all at once
I saw it. Of course, it's how you inch up to a cliff. The pull of the
cliff. He didn't fear heights. Forget duality and the broken dialectics
of striptease and musical chairs. He wasn't saying shit. He knew it,
everyone else knew it. Hard-core monist : he was afraid of this one
thing, this only thing : this everything : this falling. And his face
matter-of-fact : "I know I'm not getting far, but, *I*'m not falling for it."
I thought, that's us, all of us, even pedal to the metal, passing uphill
around a curve at night. That's still us. The illusion of motion. Speed's
the most popular kind of noise we know. It's why the more time you
think you've saved the less time you feel like you have. Volume is a ruse
for the bone-deaf. The way speed is a lie told by the stuck-in-the-mud.

xiii

Open on the table in the sunlight, I glimpsed his file one day, written
in the doctor's hand on the pad . . . "Patient exhibits great care to
avoid, what he terms, a 'potentially catastrophic loss of altitude.'" I
know my mouth was wide open. And I could hear this wild laughter
coming from across the common room.

on fire   *over the rocks on the breakwater*
    with his body

Interview : "Put Your Hand in the Hand" :

January 30, 1979 : St. Louis, MO

He told me : "After church   I remember when I was little asking my
grandmother about why my hands made songs sliding down the rail of
the stairs

that's just about it   but   I can see her face get   strange   I can see
her face get serious before she turns towards me   I hear her say :
how's that?

And me : why do my hands make songs
                on the rail when I go down the stairs

And she : which stairs   baby?   And me : does it matter grandma?

And she looking down that serious way   just over my head
and down the street   angels strolling in broken circles on the
sidewalk   shadows of angels in fish nets   angels leaning into the
shadows of cars on the curb : "yes it does   child   yes it does"

ii

Most people remember him playing. Singing. Few remember, now, that he never wanted to sing. And, everyone recalls his laugh.

I see him sitting there in a room full of talking people, head cocked slightly, a look of something just short of tender seriousness in his face. Face like sunshine thru an open window. It's what his face had become. And I can see a kind of wondrous confusion playing his eyes and mouth. Hands rubbing up and down on his thighs, looking from face to face across the room.

He'd watch a conversation like a tennis match. If you spoke to
someone behind him, he'd dodge to the side. That's it. What he'd
become : wondrous and confused

I can see him like that. Just like that at the piano, face in some kind of
tennis match with his hands. Singing : "giving up is so hard to do . . ."
or "thank you for being so good   so good to me . . ."

And he'd say   "I wish you all could hear the music going on just
behind these songs   right . . . here   music : a playground full of
shadows with skinned kneecaps and, *there*," and he'd hit some kind of
twelve fingered chord, "and, *there*, somewhere off in back of what I'm
doing. Cause you know? What am *I* doing *here*!?"

Listening Notes : After Shock Therapy :
Mercy Medical Psychiatric :

November 7, 1973 : Chicago, IL

Deafening   I sit with my hands weightless on the keys
goddamn   I could sit like that for hours   Debussy said he never
wrote down a line until just before it disappeared
I tried it : Jesus, it hurt at first   but   it's strange   got to where

I thought he'd jumped the gun   got to where I could wait   I mean
really wait   sit and deny nothing   watch it above   below   watch
it and numbed to nothing   and wait   and watch the whole line in
my head

vanish   and wait and not flinch an inch   and the glow gives itself to
the dark

ii

and wait   and not write it
until I could sense it getting light behind me   and then what I wrote
wasn't the line I'd lost   they don't   don't fool yourself   they never
come back   no simple second inversions   I'd wait   and never
look   and I'd write down what I could

feel coming on   behind me as if it was right over my shoulder   I
swear I thought there were
shadows   I used to pretend they were people   a gathering behind
me   around me   but the noise became undeniable   forced   I tried
wishing they were people and the noise seemed to change

into music   but they aged quick   too quick   at one point I said to
myself   shit   if they age that fast   maybe they're dogs   I thought,
'try dropping one from the roof, maybe they're cats'   I tried giving
up   into the gathered   would-be people   I tried to be one of
them   I tried color   someone told me that if they were in oils it
would matter   maybe   seems not enough   not to me   so I gave up
on what and went back to how

I went back to this basic sense of coming-on   gathering   until I
really couldn't deny it : truth is   they weren't coming   they were
leaving   I remember the thought : what if they're leaving?   leaving
after vanishing?   and there was a sudden wind of fear   like someone
inside me inhaled the air I'd just breathed in   then solid wood   fast
ball on what those old men around Carr Square used to call '*good*
wood'   I remember them talking about Musial   Garagiola   Devil
Wells and Cool Papa Bell   a feeling like something's alive at the other
end   a long pull on a fish hooked deep

swallowed the hook   an old man told me : bottom feeders ain't like
trout   they're way too stupid to outsmart   you have to outwait
the lazy bastards   and they can wait   what in hell else they got to
do?   can you say that?   there's no bone in their mouths   no way to
set the hook   wait

boy   til you can pull the line straight thru him   wait til he shits it
out the other end   otherwise go on and be smart and quick   find
you one of them trout streams and stay clear of muddy water

the would-be gathering behind me   I was right : a vanishing   there
are no people back there   ever stared into the eyes of an
owl?   something comes back at you   we don't have a word for it and
won't find one   caged or not   bars matter nothing   the eyes stare
straight thru to the bone   beyond the bone   straight thru to what
bone becomes

eyes full of nothing you can name

I wouldn't write it til I could see it like that   with no regard for what
it is   was   I'd wait til it moved again   and then I'd write it en route
to what it'd become   that's how I taught myself that there's no one
thing and *that* thing is no thing   that's how I concluded that   if 8
contains 7   it also contains 9   so   I'd watch 8 and write 9

v

I could see what the sight of an owl leaves out

straight on   no angles in the eye of an owl   power gathered up
in night-vision   an intelligent silence high in a barn   that's all it
is   silence gathered : vanished from the beam and one pass thru the
dark   something else stirs in the hay   there's symmetry in

and behind the eye   if it sees energy   it means to let it loose   and
be gone

                                    long gone

          he's on fire   he climbs over the rocks   *and*
opens the blue

III

I remember playing a game called "Hide and Go Seek,"
where a group of kids would hide while one kid would
close his eyes and chant :

> Last night the night before
> Twenty-four robbers came
> knocking at my door
> I got up ; let them in
> Hit them in the head with a
> rolling pin

— DONNY HATHAWAY

"A Song for You" : A Conversation :

October 26, 1975 : Chicago, IL

Jesus Christ, they call their lovers — Jesus Christ they call their lovers
partners. I hear them whisper : "professional commitments . . ." I hear
them whisper : "limited liability." I hear them whisper from their
urns : "to what will love not stoop?"

Look, call it what you want, after you broke the window,
you know what we had? A week
in January with a big old air-hole in the window.

But, can you breathe?

Yes, thank you. For fear of further wasted breath, can we talk?

About what?

How about we start with the day you walked, as you say, thru me and
into the sun?

That door swings open into the dark room and brass hits blare
bright wood in the floor.

Brass hits? Try freezing your ass off. You came straight out of the bath
walked past me and stood ankle deep in the snow. You say you can't
stand it lately. Then, you say nothing. You sit at that piano with your
back to us.

I'm looking for you.

Christ! Fuck you. Try looking *at* me! Turn around.

Presto. Cold hands on my back and a dance on the wall. Sunlight thru a broken window caught in a glass pot of boiling water. I see you there. I aim up and away, sight breaks up and to the left at the surface. Blue flame under glass.

Where does it stop? There are people who talk to each other, you know?

Is that a joke? Try listening to what they're saying. And where does what stop? The glass. I don't know. Fire. The blue . . . I don't know what to play. I find an image and play it. I can see it, there, go from open to closed. Window to mirror. I can hold down a chord and watch it go back and forth and follow it until the wire dies. And I can sit there and almost hold myself in the death of that last wire. As a rule, I know an octave equals half the length of the one below. As for rules . . .

After that, I can feel it go thru my arms. Feathers loosed inside my limbs. I call them you. They have other names. I call them by other names. They're just about the only things I trust enough to talk to and not feel the shouting lies claiming my words like when the wind takes smoke out of your mouth. Like wind blows straight thru a burning log.

But, how many people can you find willing to be feathers in your arms?

Other than you, you mean?

Watch it smart-ass. You and the jokes?

Humor's a ruse around the stuff I'm too afraid to sing about.

And the tears?   Same.

And the pain?

High-altitude chorus in my hands. Cirrus grain in the wood. The touch that won't lie.

Where does it stop, then? How high are you trying to get? How wooden do you want to be?

iii

Remember when we were burning up on that top floor off the boulevard in August? 55th and King? Above the neighborhood, light in from all sides, all day. The baby'd go to sleep in whatever corner was dim at the moment. The day it got so hot we parked her in front of the fridge and left the freezer open. She laughed at the cold clouds falling over her. Her first real laugh.

We stuck our hands in bags of ice until they ached and covered each other's face. Open wounds under aching hands. A cold thumb in your mouth. You slipped clear slivers of ice inside yourself and looked straight thru me. Ice in your eyes.

No living thing stops. Ever. We're breeze in the tree tops. There's no point in life where the momentum ebbs and the thing rocks back like a car with bad struts at a stop sign. Things are stuck all over, yes, stopped, jammed. Smashed. Movement gone under the silent torrent. The obsession with speed. But, the action of the stop never happens. Might catch an early stage. But, no one catches the moment things stop. Think about that heat.

We'll know it's stopped when no cold fingers press into my wet temples. It's stopped when you can't hold heat and ice long enough to guide me in so I could feel them both. When hands don't ache in the summer. And you can't hold me still so still I can't tell freezing from burning or whose pulse is whose. It's stopped when you can't trust what you can't see, what can't be seen. When you won't let what you see and what you don't see disappear into each other. It's stopped when we can't anymore disappear. Stuck here in this plastic empire of action and exported graveyards. Antics. Gestures.

Maybe it stops when fear partners us
with oblivion and I call you and your name's the wrong name
and you say don't ever touch me like that again.

When we get tired and agree without agreeing. When we use their words and forget we have our own hands. And what they're for. When we've started to draw straws.

iv

Here's where it stops. I say : "can't you feel the dancers move and jeer just behind your brain?" And, you say you don't see it that way.

Or won't. And that day, effortlessly, becomes everyday : no one sees that happen. You say : "no, I know they're there. But, I can't anymore convince myself that they're worth the trouble." And me : "those dances are us." And you : "Tell them to go to Hell."

But, aren't we getting further and further behind? Aren't we losing track of things? I mean real things? I mean real life.

Interview : Graveyard Shift :
Carr Square Projects :

July 20, 1980 : St. Louis, MO

You say you're looking for people to talk to you about Donny
Hathaway? What do you want to know? I never knew him or nothing
like that.

Did he live around here or something? Right here, don't say? I don't
know nothing about that. I'm from down South, moved up here five
years back. Florence, Mississippi.

I know his music, heard him sing once. I heard somewhere, years ago,
he was sick? I don't know nothing about that either. Not sick sick,
head-sick or something.

I went with my first wife and saw him play a little club in Chicago one time. Forget the name of the joint. He came in wearing a sweater and a thick gold chain around his neck. I remember that. And, of course, that hat. Look, it wasn't no big deal. He might as well have been singing on the El platform. Club wasn't nothing but a rib joint with a bar and a stage. He might as well have been singing out on 63rd St. Crowd full of black faces. Tired faces. Faces that *look* their age, Jim. We'd all been smoking drinks from before he left to come to the club and play I suspect. Most of the people pretty high by the time he got on. High and Tired. Kind of place where high and tired rhyme, you know?

Women in the audience would call out to him when he'd pause.
Other women would answer *them*. Men didn't say a word. I know I
didn't. The women'd have themselves a ball, a party, almost like they're
watching themselves on stage. Not the men. He'd take your life like
you knew he took his own life. He'd wrap it around his fist and lay it
up side your head. It's that simple :

I'm just trying to be somebody —

He'd stare straight at your life and see it like you can't and sing it like
you don't. And there's a bunch of good reasons why you don't hear it
sung like that, too. I bet there are, anyway, cause I don't know them.

I brought it all home to you baby —

But, I've thought about it since. What it comes down to is he'd stare
right at it. Black in this hellhole of a world and don't understand why?
Woman in a funk and don't know why? Baby's crying in your arms
and her mother's gone out the door and down the street. A pair of big,
rough black hands and this little baby. And that hurt coming at you
cause you know *you*'ve been down the street with the baby crying and
you know *why* you went down the street.

He'd sing a door swung open into an empty room. I remember : 'Little woman . . . hello.' There's that hit song, now, 'Never Too Much.' You got that right! Should be 'Never near enough and it ain't even close . . .' You know? Should be 'nobody's got enough less he's on his way to jail and plenty on their way to jail and don't have shit and ain't never going to have shit.' That's the long and the short. The nut *and* the damned shell, Pete. Should be 'enough already, shit!' But, that ain't going on nobody's radio, is it? He'd sing it. One way or another, he'd sing *that*. Then he spoke into the mic and he'd pronounce the words exact. We didn't expect that. Exact. Titles of songs, who wrote them, he said, 'may God bless you all . . .' He sang some kind of 'put your hand in the hand of the man . . .' stuff next. But, he got back to 'never near enough . . .' Half the time, you can forget the words, he hummed a verse and had half the room in tears. Then he'd sing and wag his head and peel back his voice til it was raw flesh in the wind. Black flesh, black wind.

v

It's that simple. And he'd sweep down take all that up in a simple line
and blow it out like a mouthful of smoke over birthday candles.

Simple as that. It was black life. I ain't no philosopher. He sung you
a black man's life. You knew cause you'd lived it. You'd even sung it
yourself. But, not like that you didn't sing it. And not like *that* you
didn't live it, either. Did I say how he'd look your life right in the eye?
Simple stuff. "Little girl, *why* did you go?"

I know he sold records to all kinds of people. Played in Europe. That shit don't mean nothing. It was black life. You look around. Turn the camera around and around down here. Right now or come back in an hour. Come back in ten years. It's black life. They can listen if they want. Anybody. People can do anything they want. But, *that* was black life he had in his mouth. His hands. His foot on the pedal. A black man's life. There've been others. Curtis. Marvin. Stevie. They all had their own trips. But, Donny stared your life right in the eye. Bobby Blue Bland does it some. Al Green did it a bit. You all probably know this already. Don't know who you're going to show this to? Chances are they already know all of this cause it ain't nothing complicated he did. Just stare right at a black man's life. Most of your viewers won't do that. Most of them probably don't come around down here no ways. Some may *live* around here. And I tell you what. No one down here looks their life in the eye. Not and lives to tell about it they don't. Some do and end up with a face that looks like this busted-up curb right here. Maybe a woman might look at a black man's life. She might stare over the fence. His woman might look. And tell you *all* about it you can bet on that. Love, Jim.

vii

And, I remember at one point he stopped the band and asked politely if we could be quiet and applaud if we liked at the end of each song. There was a roar of laughter. He wasn't laughing, I remember that.

I guess I've gone on too long. You'll probably cut this up some kind of way like they do on the news channel til it sounds like I'm saying the opposite of what I'm trying to say. That's pretty much what happens whenever anyone down here says something into a camera. Surprised they didn't send some blood down here for the scoop. You got guts, I'll give you that. "Ha." Made you flinch.

So, that's what I heard. I sat there high as a kite and watched that
stocky brother sit at the piano and stare my life down. He opened
his mouth and what came out was things none of us looked at. Life.
I drove home the next day and went to work that night. That's where
I'm headed right now. I clean the killing floor at the stockyard after
second shift. Used to be three shifts of killing, you know. But, the
bosses decided to get the place clean each day and give all the killing
a chance to blow out of the air. That's our job. Scrub the killing away,
they say the scent spooks the animals. Or, maybe it was the union said
the constant killing spooks the killers. So I'm not a killer anymore.
Never was much of one, never got used to it. Now, I take a squeegee
like the one you use at a gas station but bigger, and push blood into
the gutters. I hose down the bricks. I love the way the place looks
when I leave in the morning. All those clean bricks. Wasn't too long,
later on, I hear he's dead.

Didn't hear how. Didn't need to. I said to myself and my partner, Jay Brown, who works third shift with me. Now Jay Brown was a real killer. Worked the floor ten years, before lunch, he'd wash his hands by holding them under the spigot of blood. One day, he said he'd had enough and joined the third shift cleaning crew. I said, 'what are you doing here in the middle of the night, Jay Brown?' He said, 'I had enough.' That was about the last thing I heard him say. Shoot, might have been the *first* thing I'd heard him say? Anyway, that night, I said, 'I knew it. I knew it. I knew it.' I said, 'I could have told you that sure as shit sure as I'm standing right here on this blood streaked brick right now.' I said, 'don't nobody stare a black man's life down and get away.' And, Jay Brown, he didn't even turn around from mopping the blood into the gutter. He heard me, though. I know he heard me. And I said it right. Anyone who says he did, he's either back from the dead, bleeding inside and on his way, or he's nothing but a goddamned lie. Go ahead and bleep that one out if you want. Got a match?

A month later Jay Brown said his cousin, Kick, had got him a job up in Chicago. Laborer with a small crew of bricklayers. He said, 'they go from town to town and there ain't supposed to be no blood on this job.' I said, 'sounds good to me, Jay Brown. Sounds good to me.' Ain't seen him since. As for Mr. Hathaway, leave it up to the radio, watch. They'll make a Christmas singer out of him. They'll have my man coming down the chimney. Sugar plums. Thanks for the light. Good luck with what you're doing.

the blue with his body

Interview : Everything Is Everything :
"I hear voices   I see people . . ." :

February 5, 1979 : Brooklyn, NY

What he'd do with an empty staff   we'd get there early   write out
our parts or half of them   shit   we'd be high mostly   we got so we
didn't half care what we wrote   knew he'd change it all
anyway   that's how we noticed it first

the different voices   he'd sit at the keys   play one part and sing
another   then switch
after a while   the voices started to change   he'd switch them and
they'd stay switched
then your part wouldn't come back in the same voice   and him
furious cause you missed the mark

one night   it was just him and me and Arif in the studio   I asked
him about the voices and he got real quiet   said he didn't know any
of them   but   far back as he could see he'd heard his own voice
against a kind of chorus   said it's why he never wanted to sing at all

he could play the melody   and do whatever he wanted with
it   but soon as he started to sing   the voices appeared   in every
pause   said he never remembered wanting to sing   not even as a
child   on stage   voices coming out of his mouth   voices behind
him   all those faces out there beyond the lights

iii

far back as he could see   he saw audiences   staccato
people   stomping people   cry and shout when they're
happy   that's what his grandmother said   they just getting
happy   it terrified him   this happiness   stomping and clapping
and sweating   first lecture he attended at college   at Howard   a
music lecture   prof talked about a frenzy   call and response   called
it   played a tape : he knew the tape

lied : he could hear claps like gunshots   blue sparks in the dead of
night   blurry lights and head lamps on a chariot   scythe blade and
pendulum chant   voices
rising up to the edges of his ears   voices looming overhead   waves
over the winter breakwater at the lake

water freezes in midair and smashes   ice-blades on the concrete   far
back as he could see   this is what quiet meant to him   a chance for
voices to tell him to "sing it"   and he sung it out of sheer
self-defense   until he couldn't hear the difference   til he'd
disappeared into the waves

iv

just once   he said   he'd like to play against the quiet house   too
late   maybe if I'd learned in some soundproofed room   say
in Vienna   and not on those stages   truth is music's always
been a haunted house   Un Hiver a Majorque   Arif showed
him the tapes   said he could record singing over a chorus of
himself   which   let's face it   had to be about as bad   no   it had
to be worse

nude   he's on fire

Listening Notes : "Fine and Mellow" :

April 1, 1955 : St. Louis, MO

On the way down Washington to New Jerusalem in the dusty, early morning light. The kind of morning in early spring when the daylight, diffused, offers no clue about the position of the sun and the sky looks like a damp slab of concrete. As if it should have pillars. Dawn and high noon, same wet slab. He thinks, if it rains, it'd have to fall as gravel. Looking at his feet appear in front of him as he walks and kicks pieces of asphalt and sidewalk, he says to himself, "it must have rained hard last night." He heads on, kicking pieces of the sky into the street. One of the angels stopped him at the corner. Said you're out late there, little man. And he : naw, up early. And she : care to bet?

She turned and the edge of an unbuttoned summer blouse brushed his face and loosed something clear and brassy in his mouth. He swallowed it back and followed the scent of smoke and sweat as if it were a towline through the weather-whipped door and up the stairs. The blouse wasn't unbuttoned. Didn't have buttons. Fastened with a purple jewel at the top, it fell slightly open, moved as she turned showing him something gold-speckled over brown skin. As it swept past his eyes and through his nose, the gold and brown switched places in him long after she'd turned and headed inside. Follow the sun, he thought. Flight onto dim light, the next landing-shadow up onto a sagging last flight. He never once moved his legs. He thought this must be how people move in the big, two-floor store downtown that has the power stairway. He knew, somehow, this was all ok if he didn't move his legs. The steps disappeared beneath his chin, he could feel himself fall through open space. The street, his porch, the church spun in his brain as if disappearing down the drain. Burnt match sticks. The totally new, effortless, motion in the hallway revealed his life, everyone he knew again and again, to him. The performers on the corner. A wink, an ace up a sleeve. A low voice whispered behind his ear : "Which card you want, Little Rock? Where's the pea? Nothing but a thing, Chief, everyone's a winner."

There were hands all over his body. They moved over his unmovable legs as he rose over flights of stairs that, for once he thought, deserved their names. *Flights.* Then, in the room, blinds pulled. The room dark save one swath of light that cut across the floor, caught the edge of a round table and shot up the wall. The line of light moved once, a cat broke the beam and stopped. When its tail switched, it stirred up galaxies. Motes like pin pricks made the thin column bristle in his eye. An experiment : even with both eyes shut tight, he knows when his head turns past the column of light. Unexpected result : with eyes closed, he sees the dust motes magnified thousands of times. As if, when they're closed, his eyes turn into microscopes. Or telescopes? Red and blue and purple, he can see that some revolve faster than others. Event without cause : he only hears the cat purr when his eyes are closed.

iv

She : you know I've heard you sing. Now and again, when I feel like wearing a hat, I come and listen to the music. And he : you mean down at New Jerusalem? And she : umhmmm, you've got a fine voice. Already a *fine* voice. The breath from her *f* caught the lobe of his ear, each hair on his arms stood up and he felt like he was moving again but figured he wasn't because, unlike on the steps, everything else stayed where it was. And he : I don't like to sing much. I don't like to make noise. People tell me it's a joyful noise, but, I don't know about that . . . But, I know I can fix songs. I know how to fix them on a piano. And she : shhhh. After a long pause : how old are you? And he : nine. And she : is that all? Yes, that's all. Nine. And she : well you come on over here number nine.

v

And she sat him in a chair at a small, marble-top table with a wrought-iron base and pulled the other chair around behind him. He put his arms on the table. For an instant, he could feel the cool of the marble through his sleeves. And she started to hum a song. Part of the song was "Safe into the Arms of the Lord," and his left hand took G-minor and slid the seventh down the smooth surface of the cut rock. And her hum turned itself over itself in some kind of way. The voice in his ear moved inside itself. It sounded to him like it moved thru his head like how your leg slides under covers to find a cool place in the summer sheets and some invisible blur follows behind like how the shadow of your warmth bleeds away from one place and collects under your leg in another. The way you wake up face down in a pillow and turn over to find a new morning on the ceiling full of light. Her hum moved like that as if she'd turned her tongue over in her mouth and turned that close hum into some kind of far away moan. And he stopped. And she put her chin down on his shoulder : what's this sound like to you? And he : I don't know?

And the hum got closer and the moan farther and he felt two fingers trace the new line of his hair across the back of his neck and up to his right ear. Then, the finger went back down and up the other side. And the hum rolled around with its mouth closed and the finger returned warmer and wet to the touch and up to his ear. And the hum turned itself over again and the moan felt much closer than the hum had ever sounded. He could feel her breath cool the line on his neck. Closed his eyes. The cat idles in the dark and he saw his hands like some old pianos have mirrors behind the keys. He could see the reflection of his hands. The reflected hands moved and he could almost hear what they'd sound like on keys, but his arms had vanished from the tabletop and he felt himself tumble backward. When he tried to put his feet to the floor he found that someone had snatched the linoleum out from beneath him like a magician snatched the tablecloth without so much as a flutter in the bright, wet eye and open keyhole of the candle. The whole room folded into that column of light, stirred into swirl and frenzy by the pulse of a cat's tail. And he thinks : if I had an ear, it'd be where all this disappears. It'd be how the whole room, the hum and the moan and the cat and the dust entered my missing, singing body.

And, the breath was humid on his ear and cheek and he felt fingers like splinters of light trace his shoulders and down his arms and off the tips of his middle fingers. The splinters brushed back and forth, once, over the backs of newly appeared hands and went off the cold rock like it was the edge of the world. She bit his earlobe lightly and flicked it once with the tip of her tongue and he felt cymbals crash through his limbs and the moan stopped and a rush of silence nailed his feet to the boards beneath the floor.

viii

And she : If you don't know, it's because you don't know what pleasure
is. Or *say* you don't. But you do. Don't you? You know. At least
you know now. Don't you? For now. But what pleasure is, little Mr.
Number Nine, won't stand still for you. For anyone. But, from what
I've heard from you, wearing my hat on those few mornings, *least* of
all for *you*, Brother Pitts. It'll be hide and sneak, for you, busted in and
face to face, back to back and kicked like even the catch-can can't be
kicked. Pleasure is the sound of an open, opening that somehow turns
into a need, needing. And back. Everyone's afraid of pleasure. Take
it from *me*. Many think they'll have to pay something to someone
for every moment, for every ounce of it. Take it *from* me. Say what
they want about this and that, most are afraid, and should be, cause
they think when the bill comes up due, past due, they guess they'll
have to pay with pain. You won't get this now, my little lovely little
man, but you'll meet flocks of people, crowds, herds, who've whipped
themselves half-starved and crazy cause they think they can buy off
what they owe pleasure with stuff like, say, anger, or humor, instead of
going on ahead and paying up in pain.

When did you start singing? Can't remember, always, I think? Umm, well, that's what you've got in your voice. That's what won't sit still. Moves when you don't. Something that won't be explained. I've heard your voice go from pleasure to pain and back; it can pause in either and never stop being both. You don't know anything about this, do you?

Nope. Could you do like that with your finger again?

Your voice knows more than you do. Already does and always will.

Like what does my voice know? Like what pleasure, pain, anger are. Like that they either don't exist at all or they're all the same thing. But, and this is what's got everyone's snip in such a tight grip, *events* occur. Things happen. Things like prisms that split light into rainbows, light into color, get it? Fine. But, see, things are made of *other* things. And those other things of other things themselves. A finger that, say, hummed a moan in your faraway ear. A finger that's my flesh, sure, but a finger you can't feel until it's yours, too. Prisms inside prisms. One day it'll bear you up. Colors inside colors. Another, it'll *tear* you up. And back to white inside *that*. And, one day, you won't feel it at all. And you'll want to know why and there's no reason why and so you'll try to remember which was which and when. Then, memory shows itself: shafts of light from an antique mirror thrown from the balcony. Shafts made of other shafts. One day, it'll wear *you* out. The earth spins under the mirror as it falls. And there's your voice that knows *event* means *once* and once, always, means *now*. Voice. And now followed, like a tongue touched to a finger-tip, by —

By event?

Ah, there, see? And people are going to want to hear your voice, little man. But they're going to do just about anything they can to keep themselves from knowing what you know. And so will you Brother Pitts. And so you will.

So will I? But, I just told you. See, so, I *do* know —

Slow down, now. Jesus, you're quick. Nono, see, I'm talking about what *you* know. What *your* voice knows. All of that, you see, has so very, very little to do with anything *I* have to say. I can hold your coconut-colored head in my lap and stroke you til tomorrow. I can split your scalp. And, either one, the difference or not, means a nothing-seed in the core of nowhere til you make it yours. And no one knows how they do that. No one can hear their own voice in the mirror. Composers. No one can tell you how to do that. And nothing, *nothing*, can stop you from doing it. That's the kicker in the snicker.

You're doing it right now. It all goes in and that's part of the pain, the forecast of the pain, but, the beauty is just around the corner. The beauty is that when you've made it, me, yours, it's not mine anymore. I'm not mine anymore.

Til I give it back?

There you are, hmmm. That's part of the beauty as well, sphere spun in a world of circles. Pearls. Kind of like turning the mirror around and scratching your own back with both hands, right? But, no, the real beauty is that you don't give it back to *me*, little man, you give it to someone else. The real beauty's beyond your reach. Picture a scene of everyone giving what they've made of others to others still and I think you'll know why 'anonymous' is the most beautiful word we have that won't fit in any song. Say it three times under your breath. Anonymous. That double tongue-touch that ends as a hiss on your lips. Anonymous. It hisses like pure pleasure and trails through your head like a mouthful of French wine. You say it.

Anonymous?

Can't put that word in a song. Cause it's already a song. It's *all* the songs, baby boy. A symphony where finger-stroke and fist-strike change places every time the lights come on.

But, because no one knows any of this or because they do, it doesn't matter, they're going to flock to you and they're not going to know why. Some of them *will* know, at least a step or two of their own, and they won't want to know. So they'll lie about . . . They'll lie about everything. Memory's a mirror in the hallway. The earth doesn't spin. The city's not just a bunch of dust glued in place. You pick it. You'll hear it all. They'll say they come to hear you sing to *forget* their troubles. And then there'll be you, in a room that moves when you move, with a voice that's a search from the next open opening inside of all the will and won't and will and won't want and won't and won't will and need and don't want and need and can't have. And need and can't have. And need and can't have. Voice a search for an opening between need and can't have and have and can't need til your teeth burn, a flame in your ear and sunburn on your tongue. Voice. Something stayed inside, flame sucked breath from beneath the door. Voice. Something leaned back, feet on the sill, something blew the grimy pane clean out the window frame.

And he : Is that why I don't want to sing? Just fix up them songs instead? And she : Maybe yes, maybe no. And she whispered it, close, in his ear til he couldn't remember who said it. But, here's what I know, *take* it from me. People come to me and don't know why, too. Sure as I'm sitting here, proving to you that you know goddamned well what I sound like, you *know* what *I* am. And, you know you're going to sing. You're going to sing your black, brown, and beige life away, boy. Sing the one, slow-way up and all the fast-ways down. Sounds and you'll say they're voices you hear. Clouds in the street, in your bed, cut by sunlight and you'll teach yourself to call pleasure by its name : people beneath your hands. Maybe some people got it like faucets that turn off and on? I don't think so, but, that's fine. Mellow, you know? For others, though, even when it's off, shut down, rusted through and broken back down into dust . . .

And he : . . . it's *still* on. And she : you said it. So, don't let any of them wish-they-were windbags where you're headed tell you that you don't know what it is. And he : what do you mean where I'm headed? And she : Tell 'em you're a fine and mellow fellow, little man number nine, and even when he's turned off he's on.

he climbs over   and

opens

IV

I recall one time, maybe a month into us being roommates, he came home when I was playing Miles Davis's *Porgy and Bess* album, the one with the elaborate arrangements by Gil Evans. He sat on the couch and listened for a while. Then he began moving the needle around from cut to cut. After that he sat down at the keyboard and rearranged the whole thing as it was playing. He stretched the chords and made it all his own. It was an incredible experience.

— LEROY HUTSON

Interview : Front Porch : Carr Square :

January 25, 1979: St. Louis, MO

Little Donny Pitts? Sure, sure. Tell you one thing, didn't matter to me one way or another if the boy was saved, damned, born on borrowed time, or bought on layaway. I knew him. I could see he had a whole lot of things going on inside. More than that rickety church he was going to could vouch for. I'll tell you that. And I knew what women like his grandmother said about me, too. But, this ain't about them, is it? What'd he do this time, disappear? Ain't seen him in years.

He lived across the way, down there in Carr Square. Used to come sit on my front porch. I'd give him a jackknife and a stick to whittle along with me. He'd chip away and smell the greenish wet wood beneath the bark. He'd steal glances at me out the corner of his eye like he's trying to count the change the Devil's got in his pockets or something.

ii

He'd always take his hands and sweep the shavings into neat piles. His
shavings now, he never touched mine. Didn't say much. I'd catch him
staring out of the corner of his eye.

And me : don't you look at me sideways   boy   til you know
something   like how hard it is to sit up here all day and do nothing

And he'd go back to his stick. You could see all the things he'd never
say. Lightning branches across the right side of his skull. One day, bolt
blue, told me   Said   "I know something"   Said it felt like there
were electric hands inside his head playing his brain like all it had
was busted keys. Playing his brain like that broken down piano in the
basement of New Jerusalem on Seventh Street.

iii

There were days when he'd just stand on the steps and run his hands
up one stair rail and down the other. He'd kind of squirm like he had
to pee or something. And there were muscles in the jaw that'd pull his
mouth to one side   no one could deny it

there from the get   changes in person midsentence   like if you
switched key halfway thru
running down a scale   Oh   I know something about music myself
now

he'd say something like that lightning stuff   and pause   and I'd ask
something and someone else would answer back   we'd talk like that
and I might not see the other kid for weeks   told me one day that
he couldn't even look at a piano without hearing people's voices all
scattered and broken up   said in school they told him not everybody
hears the same things he does   and he learned not everybody can
just walk up to the keys and put the voices back together   like they
were   'natural' he'd say   the changes in that little boy's voices could
make hair on your arms straighten up   and sooner or later   he'd
always come back

told me there's a man in a wet black raincoat always follows him
around   said he calls him Mr. Soul   And me : what if it's not
raining?   And he : coat's always wet, shine so bright in the sun til it
liked to hurt your eyes   said he calls the girls down on Washington
Avenue 'angels'   said the man waits outside the church for him   said
he waits outside too when he goes in where the angel takes him   said
he asks questions even he can't hear about what he does inside in the
dark with the angel   what am I going to say   I knew that angel
before she was an angel   in fact   I knew *her* before she was a *she*

I know this much   no one taught the stuff he'd learned   so no one
knew how to follow him   no one   not even he could follow some
of that stuff   to a point   yes   beyond one of those twists   one of
those changes in key   you can forget it Sam   'natural' he'd say   if
you ask me   it's more like how to squeeze water from a rock   no
denying it though

that boy had him one powerful gift

                                        for shrubbery

I used to think   knowing what he knew   he was going to good-
and-damn-straight need that gift and some more on top of that one
used to think : go ahead Little Donny   you keep talking to the man's
got a wet coat in the bright sun   you beat your way the long way
around the burning bush

Listening Notes : "yesterday suddenly
suddenly yesterday" : Letter to the Shadow
Hanging Over Me : Mercy Medical Psychiatric :

February 27, 1973 : Chicago, IL

Mr. Soul, you're not real. The first doctor said it again and again. Asked me "have you ever touched him?" I said of course. Said I bumped shoulders with you three times a week. Asked me "how did it feel?" Said you know said it felt like someone pulling on my shoulder from behind, like someone trying to turn me around to go at least to look the other way. Asked me "so he bumped you from behind?" Said no, from in front. Asked me "but, then, if it felt like someone behind?" Said that's the way it felt you asked me how it felt. Told me, answers like that are no way to get myself better no way to get myself out of here no way to get myself back on the street. Thought to myself, is that better? Said, I figured not.

Then another doctor. Asked me if you were always waiting outside. Said yes. Waiting for me outside the hospital? Said yes. Right now? Yes. Asked me "how do you know?" Said I can see you leaning on that light pole. Asked me how I could see you outside when I was inside? Said good question. Asked me what you were wearing? Said always the same thing, thick black raincoat. Asked me why the black raincoat on a bright day? Said good question. Asked if you ever talk to me? Said once. What about? Said kids. Strange, said when you spoke to me, you didn't touch me that day and I couldn't see you at all. She asked me, then, if you'd never spoken before and I couldn't see or feel you that day? Asked me how did I know the voice was yours? Said damn same way I know hers is hers. Asked, "but, you see me when I talk?" Said "you don't." Said "talk." "Then, when I ask questions?" Said yes of course. But, said "you don't use *your* voice to ask questions." Said her voice is in her hands. Said I watch her hands. It's in the hands. Asked me, "but, you said you didn't see him that day?" Said, right but I felt him. Asked me, "but, you said he didn't touch you that day." Said right. Asked me, then, "how did you feel him?" Said you were there, talking to me, holding my daughter on your knee. Asked me, "but how did *you* feel him?"

iii

What can you say to that?

That's when it got away from me. Can't recollect the details, but, the vermillion spirals, still crystal clear in front of my eyes. Angry. Look what kind of questions are these anyway? Sounds like a conversation that's been broken on the rack between pillow talk and an autopsy report. You want to know what kind of fissures there are, these days, between pure physical futility and the emotional audacity of our simple presence in the world? If that's it, ask that. Give up the gift for burning shrubbery. That game's my middle name. That game, beating around the bush, shrubbery, is how I taught myself how to learn.

And I said learn. I said it again to myself : learn. But, both times, I heard my own voice say it clearly to her : burn.

And, I'm through playing *that*. There's no simple thing to say about his tone of voice. I have songs of it. A song for how to fall down. I could fall down right here. I could fall down closer to you, close to you and pretend I'm there the way, up close, flame pretends, for a second, it's made of fingers. The way, the same way, up close, love pretends it's made of flame. Am I wrong? "The closer I get to you," the more you vanish into moonlight in the rain on the wet pearl slopes of an accident waiting, no begging, to happen. Is it fingers or flames that touch tips to slopes in your accidental needs?

The ones you touch. The ones only you can touch. The ones you'll die if no one else can touch.

iv

Songs of *this*, Ms. Doctor-here-to-cure-*me* in your four-hundred-
dollar underwear. There's no cure for *this*. The real question is how
long can a room last with two people in it? You want to know if
he was, as you say, 'really there'? But, are you really here? By dint of
what degrees? How long can the room last without someone pulling
fingernails out of the quiet, without a prayer to tears from unshed
biographies of complete strangers. Are they here?! Who dug
the moat?

V

Turn around, look at this big empty room, three windows perfectly placed in the wall. Breeze in the grass and the blue cut by those silent, rusted trees. I could fall down right here and not say a word about what's wide awake under the bridge of your drawback. We could talk about how four hot showers a day can help you dodge the cold silver stream coiled up on its hind legs in the back of your brain. About that empty, untouched, selfless self living its life in back of what's burning you from behind your eyes — but, it's not about you is it? It's supposed to be all about me, right, me and that invisible man in the coat holding my baby girl in his lap and talking to me about pure beauty and the horror holding on to horror and talking to me about beauty? Then, I recounted for her our conversation about aesthetics.

and you : remember me?
and me : of course

and you : she's beautiful
and me :

and you : congratulations on the family, man
and me : ok

and you : you've been busy   you know I have two kids myself
and me : ok

and you : yeah and they're just about the same age as yours
and me :

and you : ain't that a trip?
and me :

I could see something astir behind her doctor's mask. I could see that she'd heard something I said. I could see that I'd said something to someone in hiding. First person I'd seen in a *long* time. This meant a lot to me at the time. Man, you don't know how it is talking to none but doctors. Like dancing with ghosts. Like dancing the limbo in the pole-vault pit. But, there was someone else in the room, just then. So, I put it on the line. Said here's the truth. And the truth is on the move. You know it's moving when the pain tastes like a mouthful of brass tacks, the touch of it feels hot like the forgotten memory of fingers on your belly. Ah, let me finish. You feel this when you've seen the truth sit on horror's invisible lap. Basic, unswervable truth. So, I'm telling you this cause as far as I'm concerned the room's still here and, for once, we're alone right now. And alone isn't an empty beach. It means we're here. Here we are, alone right now. And there's a man standing out there. Right outside, right now, standing in that straight down rain the color of tempered steel. He's going to be there when I come out. It'll raining when I come out. He's got two kids of his own, bout the same age as mine. He's a cold silver drop in a boiling bucket. Flames roll up off the bottom of the bucket. Orange fingers appear and disappear, throw themselves up behind his eyes.

viii

Said you're not going to write that down?

    and she : I don't believe I will
    and me : just as well

    and she : I do believe it is indeed

You guessed it. Next day, I was there again, and there was
another doctor.

on fire   *and*

opens the blue

V

the "soul music" — and the rougher Black music :   if
someone had done that *once* — maybe it would have been
very great. But as it goes on and on in every restaurant and
every bar — It becomes something to escape from

— GEORGE OPPEN

Interview : "Sack Full of Dreams" :

June 6, 1979 : Los Angeles, CA

"Look, I didn't know him that well, ok, and I sure wasn't the only person he ever took a song from. So, if he told it to me, chances are you've heard it from others. Everyone talked about how, after he'd made it, you know, and then after he'd been in the hospital, everyone said how he'd turned away from people. Of course, there were the usual backstabbing comments. Thinks he's too good for us . . . nonsense like that. I'd say, have you ever heard him sing? They'd look at me like it's a stupid question."

ii

There are things, you know, if you've ever known *any*body . . . you
know some things about everybody. Basic things. If you've ever lain
someone down in your eyes and felt them blow like wind thru your
body. If you've felt someone so close you can feel them turn to water
beneath your hands . . . you know, so, standing next to them's like
standing in the shower?

Listen to him sing "Sack Full of Dreams" sometime. Even on record,
the whole song sounds like you're hearing it underwater. Echoes and
undulations. Feels like you could dive off a high board into the sound
and swim thru it. Liquid smoke. He told me once, that when he was
a little kid, he'd realized that that's what "Washed in the water" really
meant.

He told me these were prayers. In other words, like all others,
desperate expressions of loneliness.

iii

He'd call the hookers back in St. Louis angels. He said one used to take him up to her apartment and run her fingers along his skin and breathe in the trails of her spit on his shoulders until he could feel the paths run cool. He told me he'd learned a lot from her. Little by little, he'd noticed that people don't like change. They hate to see one thing change into another. This terrifies people. Happiness and sadness, really, make no difference to people. There are people perfectly willing to stay miserable just like there are people grimly determined to be happy. What no one seems to like is the border between them. Seems most people want clear of borders. There are people who spend all day torturing themselves to be sure they don't somehow slip over near the border of what the think might be pleasurable.

Trouble is, every *real* thing is a weave of pleasure and pain. At every level, both. Water most of all. What's the difference between water that warms and water that burns and water that saps heat from your body and turns your lips blue? Very little. Water that fertilizes fields and water that kills thousands. Exactly the same. It's as if pleasure is hydrogen and pain is oxygen. Or, maybe the other way?

He'd sing, "Can they learn, can they learn . . . to understand, the world of love. . . ." And he could sing about love and happiness and peace without ever leaving the elemental weave that joined it to pain and risk and strife. The word and the tone. Consonants and vowels. Rhythm and timbre. A singer uses vowels. When we speak, we pretend the language doesn't have vowels. Rhythm.

Kids today, they listen to "rap." Mostly, consonants. Mostly, like water with no oxygen. Even most of the singers have squeezed their tone so tight the vowels are almost gone. Like they're singing with those nose plugs you use for swimming. As if they're afraid a bug will fly in their mouth if they leave it open. We used to rap. Basically what we're doing, here, right now. Mostly sit around and bullshit. And, you're damned straight, he'd rap with you. He'd take you around the world, painting, history, music, politics. But, he knew the *rap* had to give when it came to music. Like walking into water, sooner than later, your feet leave the ground. You fly in vowels.

Try it. Try to rap "She's My Lady." Try "To love her now, is the soul thing that I'm after." Thought he meant "sole thing," didn't you? See what I mean.

We're not *talking* about words. We're talking about *lyrics*

vi

In the end, he'd become turned away. It's true. I'd see him talking
to people at 45-degree angles. By the end of his sentences, he'd turn
almost all the way around. Words would leave his mouth and he'd
wave his head like a horse in a bridle, like he was tossing something
to the side, like he was spitting out seeds. He told me it was tougher
and tougher to watch people deny the woven water and stand on
what he called 'the soul's beach.' He said it wasn't that it hurt to be
around most people, groups of people, even one by one . . . it was that
it didn't. Hurt. He said, he'd get in the middle of a group of people
talking to each other, holding wine glasses. Sitting at tables. And he
said he'd get dizzy, he'd forget which was the floor and which the
ceiling. He called it 'frantic and disorientated.' He'd say, no wonder so
many people stand along the wall, hold onto the backs of chairs, stand
like they're in a high wind. Across the room, I'd hear him belt out :
'He ain't heavy — You know ? He'd say, 'They're tumbling and praying
to stay numb so they don't feel it when they hit.'

He'd come home from parties and take a knife and cut the back of his hand. One night, I'd left with him. Came in the kitchen, I said, "What the fuck?" He said, "Oh, sorry about this, man . . ." I could see he was sorry, a little embarrassed, and then, sheepishly, "I was just checking."

Like I said, you've probably heard most of this already. And look, if you're here to talk about his death . . .

We're not here to talk about that.

Good.

Interview : "I Know I've Been Changed" :

February 8, 1979 : Brooklyn, NY

Ok. I remember in 77, down at The Last Hurrah, he called out "You Got a Friend" and then changed the key every other bar and how he raged when we said we couldn't follow him. I remember his desperate face. Hurt. And his eyes like wine bottles someone'd thrown into last night's fire pit. I can hear his voice : 'Then quit trying to follow me! If you can feel it, keep on playing. It's a free set. I'm looking for her, you all coming or not?' We said, 'Look, no one can understand what you're doing.' After the police, and the fights, and the manager and the money flying over the bar, we talked. He said, 'I need the loot for Mr. Soul, waiting for me. He's going to bump me with his shoulder and I'm going to hand him cash for the angels. And, what? As far as the song goes, I guess no one ever heard the violins introduce the theme in the wrong key in Beethoven's 8th . . . and the only ones who hear it are the one's who don't u-n-d-e-r-s-t-a-n-d. Dig?' There he paused, eyes closed, and in another voice they opened : 'You know I read the way we say 'dig' comes from 'dega,' a Wolof word for understand? And, do you know the Yoruba word for tradition, ona, means a 'fork in the road.' So, dig or don't. I remember I'd stop by the angel on my way to church, and then I'd arrive for service and the choir director at New Jerusalem, Mrs. Merdean, would say, young brother, 'your heart's been touched, and when your heart is touched, you change.'

ii

Didn't you ever walk someone home in the dark? In the rain? Did you ever swim someone home thru an underwater passage, thru the static in their brain? Didn't you ever feel like you're a completely different person wet than you are dry? Then he sang : "You wake me up, in the midnight hour and I'll tell you what I feel."

He figured he'd always be the one that looked smart to dumb folks. Looked real dumb to smart folks. All the time he spent reading, all those charts he holed away. And how many nights of concerts sung to that bare wall he'd pushed the piano up to? He wasn't stupid or smart really. Course, I've never had anyone give me a working definition of either. Seems to me, simple. If he was stupid, he couldn't have done what he did. If he was smart, he wouldn't have tried.

He told me he'd sit there and sing, he'd start the song and then he'd
leave and no one would notice. No one. Not the one hand-holding
his hand. Not smiling the smiling in his face. Not the little girl little-
girling on his lap. Not even the ones singing along. I'd seen it. He'd
snap open his eyes after "Ride On King" and say : "see that?" Two
open cycles of descending fourths and there it is : how Berg proved
Schumann was modern. Took a romantic full of broken scales to do
that. Took Grieg's A Minor Concerto in "The Ghetto" to do that.
Took what Lulu Berg sang to the wasp on Christmas Eve, 1935, to do
that. Know what Schoenberg said? Get this, said, when he showed up
to Schwarzwald, Berg was a totally vocal player, said 'it was absolutely
impossible for him to write an instrumental phrase.' Then, he'd run
off upstairs, folks in the room staring at each other in shock. You'd
hear books thudding and papers rustling on the ceiling. Then, he'd
bust back in the room, sit on the bench with some folder or book.
I remember one time, he'd gone from Ravel to Stravinsky and back
to Debussy, he concluded that Impressionism was a lie. "Ism my
ass — " he said, "by the time it had an ism, it was already on its way to
Fauvism, Cubism, Pointillisme. What it was really about was 'Nuages'
with an attitude, a human intensity, how to get full of the force,
grace, and rage of nature. Now, that's call and response. It was about
how to be open. Open to things technique would only stare at with
closed eyes. And, it was about native soil. This, when 'abstraction' was
a matter of improvised technique cracked open with pure sensation.
Understanding was on the farm team, man, with its ass nailed to the
fucking bench."

"Want proof, look here : Cézanne to Zola, 19 Octobre 1866 : 'If you
see Pissarro give him friendly greetings from me . . .' this is before
Pissarro wanted to firebomb the Louvre you dig . . . anyway, he writes
: 'I repeat that I have a little attack of the blues, though for no reason.
As you know, I don't know what it comes from, it comes back every
evening when the sun sets, and now it is even raining. It makes me
feel black.' Cézanne, 1866. Then he put his lithograph of 'Les Grands
Arbres' up on the piano and sang 'like a tree by the river, I shall not be
moved / like a tree by the river, we shall not be moved / like a tree by
the river, my man Cézanne and them gut-funky blues.'

v

This is how it started : said he'd taught his out-loud voice to follow his hands so he could play a song and the lyrics would simply flow out of his mouth. Nothing too strange about that. No. It'd sound almost as if his voice was riding the tide of his hands. Almost. See, but, he'd be singing a totally different song in his head at the same time. Not songs really, he'd play thru people and places and colors and, so he said, ferret through the broken bricks raging in his arms and legs and looking for something to say to the man with the black coat waiting. That's what his voice rode. Shoulders bump walking in different directions. Mr. Soul in the street. Always rode tandem with another voice, other voices. And after the song, like waking from a dream, he wouldn't usually remember anything. I asked if he could hear all the people out there shouting and amening and go-on-aheading at him as he sang. He looked at me a long time. Looked away. And he looked back at me for a longer time.

I just play, man, ok? And me : ok

vi

And he : But, between us. I study, too. You could say I need it. I need
it. I really need it. All of it, I know that. And, so I have to ignore the
whole damn thing. The spotlight hits me and everything goes black.
Crowd out there clueless. I need to love them. Need. And I mean
love. *Love* : let the room spin in sickness let the dance dance its sordid
veils of absence into the firelight of nonchalance. Love : I'll sing a
verse to them and chant it back to myself. Circular lyricism : 'there
are no *reasons, there* are no reasons, there *are* no reasons, there are *no*
reasons." I'll think to myself about expensive hair and all the mundane
consequences of copulation. Love birds. Love : Silent sinners and
foot nailed-in-the-floor wanderlusters. Colleagues, dear colleagues,
our last ditch hope for decorum . . . the chewed remains of what
you wished into the wind — tuned in to the main-squeeze, feature
presentation : "Gidget in Hanoi" but, first, a cartoon serial of your
After Life. Love Love Love : facile-faced, brooding and purple-plumed
and penultimate : last breath that won't cross the lips, last glance back
across the street at their backs. I'd chant, "let me off, let me off, lay me
off from my post as Chair of the Water Main and Pain Distribution.
Love lyrical as the bone-sucking onlookers in the mirror. I'd imagine
names for a whole new set of bands : Still Life : Perfect Patella and
the Broken Chain of Modifiers; Ball, Socket and the Hollow-Ass Hip
Bones; Trifecta's Groove Grove and the Grave Grifters.

Moan it. *Love*

It'd be like clockwork   the band would quit   my outside voice
would stop on a bead of sweat and the voices wouldn't even
stutter   wouldn't even pause   Over the blast of voices inside   that
blessed rage I'd come to live for and thru   over the voices
outside   inside they chant and gush our birth and death and love
and anguish flying thru the gulf stream boiled blue as pure fluid in the
spine they sing the uncharted waters of the real stuff we share   we
share what we are   over all that   And I'm in a panic to get the next
song out there   something up tempo   some ragged out worthless
airline commercial   And I'd hear some glee-filled lovely man in the
crowd call it out :

Ain't nothing but a party y'all!

he's on fire   *the breakwater*
              his body

And I'd think   Jesus, why?

And he : There'd be weeks when I didn't feel the breeze in Roberta's
voice. That lyrical, shark thru smoke in cold water tone. That playing
opossum vibrato. I couldn't live in single file. Love it, but, I'd been
in the cacophony from birth, man. From before birth. I used to
think 'shark skin' while she sang, what happens if you run your hand,
backwards, over that? I used to think : might not *have* a hand . . .
Where was I going to learn to slip thru a crack, where was I going to
learn to use a door left ajar. I was *born* wide open. Catch wind in my
mouth. Never had any training in pretending I was standing still. I
heard Baldwin talk at a school uptown. He said when he was five,
he already knew that life was hard and he was going to die. When
I heard it, it flashed in my brain. When I was five, I read that they
tried Kepler's mother as a witch. It didn't say anything about it, but,
I remember, just like that, I knew why. As a little baby, I slept in a
dresser-drawer cradle. I stood on the stoop in Carr Square watching
the cars whizz on. It was perfectly obvious to me : these people have
to believe that *they*'re the ones moving. Now, it's perfectly obvious to
me. The opposite. The science *is* the occult : earth spinning, revolving.
Sun flying or falling, spinning, gushing, and imploding all in some
keen and simultaneous, and *temporary*, balance. The whole damn
galaxy's ass over teakettle. And, all that's just the easy part around
the neighborhood. Far as I can tell, the smartest dudes around don't
know if the whole thing's a whole thing or not. And, more, don't

know if we're on our way back to the white-hot of the preblast clutch or slowing down or speeding up towards ever and ever more space between everything. Cold. And could feel the spin, I'd sing "hang on to the world as it spins around . . ." and echoes would come back in reverse.

What's that got to do wi——

Man, we don't know if we're cold or hot. And, worse, some Merlin
the Magician's wired our sorry asses to know it and watch it. Most of
human history's been about veiling it from our eyes. We're just given
the gift to be born thru the open eye of the history's hypodermic
needle.

And me : maybe some of us

And he : Ok, but which and why? And then what? Look, I used to
have patience with 'culture.' With the beauty of the blinders, the
intricate, carved, woven, painted, printed, etched, bronzed, baked,
and glazed blinders of it all. I don't anymore. I won't sing it anymore.
Or at least, not just that. I use it as what it is, what the 'we' we
recognize is : veneer. An existential drive-in. I sing it into the maze.

So, I sing the songs. I sing the songs. Veneer. But, behind the songs, I make real mistakes, I let the mind really go. I sing things no one should ever sing. And it blows the blinders off into real blindness and the night comes in like sable-black and oil-smooth fire like a symphony of neurons blown from a blood-swept stage in the back of the brain. There and not. Not and there. And back. Nothing can match all that wondrous twistery, the cables of flesh wound in the human voice. And all of it, I'm here to tell you, *all* of it leans in toward the light. Even a pinprick of light in all the blasted black and every fiber notices. They don't give themselves up, not at all. Don't have to because that's what they actually are. When all's said and sung. That's what we are, fibers in a mass, a gothic rising and choral-kind of leaning to the light. So go ahead and understand and miss the wide hitch for the thin switch.

Still, every now and then, I'd love to just hold her again and dance and have it be just that. A dance. Just us. Two. Not the man outside in the rain. Not the echo chambers that take a collision of galaxies between two and three and four people to chart. That's how they learn about blackness these days, you know, 'dark energy,' by charting the collision of galaxies. The conclusion from what I can tell : 'it's there, we don't know what the hell it is.' But, there's no getting back to that. The man said : 'Way leads on to way . . .' But, I had it. I *was* one traveler, traveling light. And, usually, it's almost enough to know I had it for a while. A real hold on a real person. Before we all split up for good, from within. You know? How kids can sit down and know each other? Language or not, no matter. Give them fifteen minutes alone in a patch of grass and they'll have themselves a game. Later it gets, the harder it is to do that. The clouds move in. Everyone's half-in, half-out of the cloud. And fear. Try as they might and most don't even do that and together becomes a real dubious term.

Another man, a poet, called all this "the shipwreck of the singular
. . ." Said it's about being numerous. I loved that — I carried his book
around with me everywhere I went for years. I felt *plenty* numerous.
Took it to gigs. Put it in the cover of a book about suicide. Put it on
the piano just to make people listen a little different. Read it between
sets. I read somewhere else what he said about black music. And, he
wasn't black, Jewish I think. It could have been my autobiography
: "over and over . . . something to escape from." But, I knew, and all
my songs tell it this way . . . it wasn't exactly like that for us. Singular.
It was bigger, lusher, closer and farther than that. Colder. It was the
shipwreck of a whole, the derailment an unprecedented plurality.

A shipwreck no doubt. But, never singular.

And me : Til now.

And he : Yeah, like a plate dropped from a balcony. Shattered and
singular. And, he's right about it, too, it ain't coming back and it
doesn't have to. Singular?

xiii

I know Webern wanted to avoid repeating himself. He was afraid of
repetition. What it implied. I think he was just afraid of Stravinsky.
But, that's for later. Maybe. He didn't want to repeat himself. He
was after the comet-tail of the singular. Dog and tail of the singular.
A whole life at work, hard at work. Boiled down into less than four
hours of singular sounds. And I'm awestruck by it, by every instant of
it. He'd mark single shots of *col legno* 'crescendo-diminuendo.' One
shot, both. Said : "the theme expresses all it has to say." Now, that's
the singular. But, that wasn't where I was coming from and I knew it.
It's an 'ism,' it's a single dot. Seurat. Already alone, too late by then.
Science had made its move on the dream of the singular. Then the real
dreams moved in on science. Kepler's mother was a witch.

They've X-rayed Cézanne canvases, man. Know what they found?
Layers of legs under legs, apples under apples, textures across textures.
Breathing forms. Here you go. Cézanne to Émile Bernard, 12 May
1904 : "One must look at the model and feel very exactly; and also
express oneself distinctly and with force." *Force*. A month before
that, to Bernard, 15 April : "treat nature by means of the cylinder, the
sphere, the cone . . ."

And me : So?

And he : Ok, but, listen to this from earlier. To Zola, 9 July 1858 :

That your brow bathed in sweat
Was enveloped by the learned vapor
Which exhales as far as me horrible geometry.
Do not believe that vilification
If I qualify
So does Geometry!
In studying it I feel my whole body
Dissolving in water under me only too impotent
efforts.

Can you believe that?!

XV

And me : I lost you, brah.

And he : Cézanne flunked Geometry! That's like Pythagoras flunking the triangle. Cause he knew it was more about sound and sun, breath and liquid, than it was about abstract forms. They sent Cézanne's mind after Pythagoras and his body came back with Heraclitus. So, he sent his body out after his brain. Cause the breath *is* sphere and cylinder. That's what's so crucial about native soil. It's not the native part, that's always up in the air. It's the damn dirt that's the point! Get it?

And me : can we try English? I mean what are you now, a farmer?

And he : It's about color, man. Tones. Look, in other words :

I used to live down the street from this old man. A vet from some old war. Two wars, I guess? Had a medal said it was written in French from one of them. I asked about the other war — He scowled at me and spit it in a whisper at me through clenched teeth : 'There wasn't no medals from the other war!' Anyway, he'd sit up on his porch everyday and whittle sticks into points. I remember one day he asked me if I wanted to whittle, I'd do it with him from time to time, you see. And one day, I think I must have said something like : 'Naw, not that again.'

And he : *Ag* . . . again? You listen here, boy. Take it from somebody should have been dead years ago. From somebody spent the second half of a stolen life doing the same thing over and over and over. One thing you don't have to worry about is doing any one thing, twice. *Again*? Another one of those words meant for people so scared of themselves they'd like to change their name every time the sun comes up.

xvii

It's the same thing. I don't have it handy, but, under the rules of color values, Cézanne said 'rage in oil, prayer in water.' Maybe what I've done is defeat the clichéd part of the cliché. Maybe I've simply found a way to mix them together.

And me : Mix what? Colors, tones?

And he : Oil and water, man, rage and prayer, what else?

Look : from Weber, 1905, "The rise of modern freedom presupposed unique constellations which will never repeat themselves." You know, so, they were right. Over and over ain't free . . . but, all the hang-ups weren't necessary either, because over and over's impossible anyway. From there it's on to how the Jacobins failed to recuperate classical form, but, you're with me up to here, right?

And me : I'll get back to you on that, D.

And he :   when?
And me :   give me forty years.

nude   *he's on fire*   *over the*   *breakwater*
                 with his body

Interview : "Little Girl, Hello" :

February 29, 1979 : Chicago, IL

He'd sing, "I shouldn't have to tell you what's wrong" and end every verse with "hello." It was a new song. It was a simple little song he'd made up in the living room after the first of the girls was born. Her crying was difficult for him to handle. In the wrong mood, very difficult for him to handle. He'd hand her to me, looking like he shouldn't have been looking, and say "You handle it." A simple little song. He said it's a song about what a father feels for a daughter. It didn't stay that way long. Other stories moved in. All that stuff about going away. I wondered where it came from. I was suspicious, I saw him changing before my eyes. For a week, I checked his pants pockets. "Lonely baby, hey it's been so lonely . . ." I'd think, I'll show you lonely. But, I knew better. He'd sing about "little woman, hello."

I could see he was desperate. Desperate to know things, always reading. He'd read things and come away with a sense of them that simply couldn't be predicted. I could see he was performing. Performances layered over other performances. He'd say we should just sit together and not talk. But, in a minute, he'd be off into some theory about art or history. Quoting from letters. Or he'd stay quiet, but I could see it all playing behind his eyes just the same. I'd say, "What is it?" And, he'd say nothing and shake his head while his eyes filled with water. What I mean is I could see he was *trying*.

iii

He was desperate *not* to know things. He'd go for weeks sailing along. He'd say, "heights ain't shit til you look down." Look, I was married to the man. *One* of those men. I love him and, really, I loved them all and I wasn't afraid of any of them. You can't imagine the gentleness. He's gone now and *I* can't imagine it anymore. The man could even shout gently. He'd become terrified of what he thought of as his cruelty. He said he loved me and I said I knew it. He said he knew he was hurting me and I said it didn't feel that way to me. And, the girls. He insisted he'd hurt them and if he stayed with it, and he did sometimes, relentlessly, he could put himself in a real state. He'd stand there and a howl would come from his mouth and no one who ever heard him talk or sing would believe that that sound came from that mouth. It did. I didn't say it, but no matter the state, the truth is that man couldn't have hurt a fly. A fly, that is, outside of himself. I'd tell him to be easier on himself and he'd nod. He'd say he loved me. He'd say it again and I'd tell him, "I know it." He'd say it again and I'd say, "I'm convinced who *else* are you trying to convince?" And, he'd nod. But sooner or later his head would begin to shake and, if they weren't already, tears would begin to drip off the tip of his nose. The man *lived* on the verge of tears. On the ledge.

iv

And he : I don't need to convince anyone, no one. I know you think I'm trying to convince myself, but I'm not. But I don't know what it is, love, and it does feel good to just say it to you. When I say it, for a moment, something stays still in the chaos. I feel good for a moment. There's no sin in that, is there? If I don't repeat it, I'm back wondering where all the pain comes from? I follow it off, as if it'll lead somewhere. Up river. Lake Victoria. Again and again, it leads to an indecipherable mess. I know where it comes from, it's wound into our flesh. It's in the fibers. But I still wonder where it all comes from. I can't stop wondering. Maybe it's nothing more than the way our brain interprets the work of producing heat. Mammals. The simple act of creating energy a body needs to exist at all, maybe that makes pain like a car in idle makes exhaust. Exhaustion.

He'd gesture toward the girls and then point into his chest then into his head. Twirling his index finger around outside his ear, "is this where they're headed?" I'd smile and say, "yes." And he'd nod until his head would begin to shake.

v

You should have seen the difference that opened up between how he'd
be at home and how he'd be outside in public. Beaten and confused
at home, sometimes, he'd walk past and it'd look to me like he was
seventy. Like he was an old man carrying a pile of sticks back to the
village. Or he'd get off into a rant about something or other. Real
contempt for people who'd come on TV and a childish, innocent kind
of contempt for politics. But, it wasn't innocent, it was the opposite;
innocence is closed off, he was open. Wide open. And, he didn't give
an inch. It was that he knew he'd fallen, he knew everything had
fallen. I think he'd come to see falling merely as the reality behind
everything. He'd say : "We're not people, we're waterfalls. That's what
it is." He'd lash out at any pretense of order, social order, political
order. He'd say : "sand castles on melted glass." These were the moods,
inside, where he'd speak in images. Me and the girls, maybe a few close
friends saw that. He'd go on these imagistic rants as if he thought the
sheer fact, the blear force, the unreal reality of falling could save him.

Afterward when the friend, usually someone in the band, left, he'd fall into me so hard it was frightening. He'd cry like a baby. Well, that's what they say but, you know, no baby cries like that. A baby's cry is nothing at all like that. He'd say he knew what he said was *all* wrong. He'd say he regretted everything he'd said. It wasn't about what he'd said. It was deeper than what; he said he regretted the saying itself. I'd say, "That's why you're a singer." And, he'd shake his head. I heard it a thousand times : "One thing's for sure, I ain't no damned singer." He'd call me before a show to go over passing tones he'd sung through a hundred times. I'd say, "Just open your mouth — "

In public, for years, he was smooth as glass. They called it success. "Take a Love Song." He called it sleep. Even people who knew him well couldn't tell that more and more of him was simply marking time until he could get the hell away from the stage, the press, from them. Audiences. Sleep. "You got to wear it. . . ." Little by little, his mask cracked and the two worlds started to mix. The confusion and despair bled their way onto the glass stage. At the same time, exactly at that time, he said he'd begun to love performing. These were the dates when he'd show up late. He'd call one song and change the key without warning. He'd break off the band and play what some reviewers ended up calling "classical pieces." And somewhere in the mess he'd be making, he'd blast off a riff, a phrase would come from that man's mouth . . . it'd leave you barely able to breathe. Sometimes almost a whole song could go that way. Some people left those performances shaken. More left them angry. The band acted either enraged or aloof but they were just scared. A few of them could feel what was happening. There were cracks and they could see light coming through them. Blind light. They weren't going near it. And, there he'd be, afterward, backstage in some kind of state of rapture. Counting out money to give to his friend outside. I'd sit back and watch him and think, "I hope he can feel every tendril of what's going through him right now. I hope he can feel every strain of color, every shadow dancing across his face." Because, I knew he'd pay for it later.

In three hours, he'd have convinced himself that "it was a travesty. A lie. A pitiful failure." We have the records. He'd say, "did you hear when I said, 'Take a strong heart and use it.' Can you believe I'd sing that!?" I'd say, "It didn't mean that and you know it." We have the records, alright. They're full of lies and failures. But, those moments are there as well. He created them. I worried that they wouldn't show up on tape. Like a vampire in a mirror, I worried they wouldn't be there. They're there alright. They'll make your hair stand up. And, he was wrong. If *he* wasn't wrong, because if anything he knew how he felt, *it* was wrong that he couldn't have held on at least a little longer to the feeling from those brilliant things that came from the cracks he'd found. He should have at least been able to enjoy them a little, for a while. A crime, really, he couldn't have held them for a little longer. Shame he couldn't turn off the thing that made them long enough to . . . to what? I don't know?

The defeated tone, the confusion, and his old-man way of walking
became clearer and clearer to people who knew him. Some people.
It was clear to anyone who didn't. From time to time, people would
hand him a dollar bill while he waited for me and the girls outside
some department store. He'd say thanks, wink, flash his gold eyetooth
and add the dollar to his roll of hundred dollar bills. Sailing along. He
never went anywhere without the roll of hundreds. Sometimes, he'd
go out at night and walk through the park sticking hundred dollar
bills in the pockets of men asleep on the benches. One New Year's Eve
he gave away 100 hundred-dollar bills like that.

One night, he came to bed and woke me up and told me he'd found
a witness. He said he'd read something that got closer than anything
he'd ever seen to what he felt like when the song takes off. He said it
was a problem with prepositions. He turned on the light. He had it
copied on a sheet of yellow paper. He kept that piece of paper with
him for the rest of his life. He had it in his pocket when he died. I
have the sheet upstairs, folded in four, the creases have worn through
almost completely. I told him over and over to type it out or rewrite
it on a piece of new paper. I told him he knew it by heart. Anyway, he
said he needed to have it just as he wrote it, when it felt like the only
thing he had. He'd fit it in with the bills. When it was new to him,
staring at him with what he'd been though a thousand times without a
name. Here's what it said, you see, I even know it by heart. It's a letter
from Alberto Giacometti, some kind of a Swiss-Italian artist who lived
most of his life in Paris, to Henri Matisse in 1947.

"It seemed impossible to grasp the whole thing (we were much too close to the model, and if you began with a detail, a fingernail or a nose, there would never be any hope of getting the whole). But if, on the other hand, if you started by analyzing a detail, the tip of a nose, for example, you were lost. You could spend your whole life on it and never get anywhere. The shape would come apart; it would be no more than particles drifting on a vast black emptiness, the distance between one side of a nose and the other is limitless as the Sahara, nothing is stable, everything eludes you."

He read it to me on that bed, that night. His hands looked like no hands I'd ever seen. He finished reading and smiled, looked at me and said, "So, that's the question?" I said what's the question? And, he went back to "Little Girl," he sang, "How long will you stay . . ." He sang it in several keys. He broke it over and between several others and his hands held that piece of paper. Then, he looked at the paper and said,

"And that's me, there. 'A vast black emptiness.' But, I was full before I ever knew I could *be* empty. It's not even the emptiness that's the point, it's the vastness. The open stretches that come out of anywhere. They open out of narrows like time-lapse blossoms. It's the sensation I feel when I sing, openings into vastness behind things. It's, it's like losing. It really is like losing. Whatever you have, you're always losing it to the vastness that's behind it, that's inside it. A vastness opening out of everything. It's what's behind the wonder in people's eyes when they say, 'I was lost.' Like the girls in the backseat, in panic, tingling and excited, 'Are we lost, Daddy, are we lost?' And, I play along, I say 'Lost? No.' But, I'm thinking, 'You're damned straight we're lost. *And*, vast. And, empty.' And, you know, there's the lost and then there's the blind-lost. And the blind-lost hate losers. Never lose. Nothing worse, if you're one of the blind-lost, than to be known as a loser. You'll do anything to win, or be mistaken for a winner. Dress like one. Walk like one. That way, you can stay blind. The blind-lost are obsessed with winning. Obsessed with not doing what they're doing. Not being where they are. Cause what they're really doing is what we're all really doing : losing. Who turned *that* into a crime?

Others who knew him well were determined not to notice any of this. Shem holding the blanket singing "Walk on By." Smiles riveted on their faces. Well, he walked on by alright. But, nothing about him makes any sense without those hands I saw that night holding that piece of paper. Singing to me from that simple little song that'd opened out into the cosmos. "Little Girl." Extremities aren't quite what he'd been after. Cause it was nothing far away. *In*-tremities is more like it. You go back and look at anything he did. Listen to it again. Imagine that piece of paper in his pocket. Pants tight on those thick thighs of his. Imagine his voice against the vastness, the blackness, that it belongs in front of. I remember him sitting on the edge of the bed, paper in hand, singing "Lonely baby" and "how long will you stay." Out of nowhere he'd, "This time!" Lost in the Sahara of a little girl's cheekbone, saying "that's me . . . a vast, black emptiness."

on fire

opens

VI

An angel whispered to me, when I woke this morning
That I would find heaven by my side —

— DONNY HATHAWAY

Mr. Soul's Listening Notes : "You Are My Heaven" :
Lakefront Hallucination :

January 13, 1979 : 10:45 pm : Essex House Hotel,
Manhattan

I had the man pegged before he was a man. I watched him from out in the rain. Remember me? "La Salle St. after Hours." "63rd and Cottage Grove." Didn't think so. He knew me, though. And him trying to convince everyone I was real. Those doctors. His band. Good luck. I knew where he was headed. Figured I'd just meet him there. I knew he was close when he got out of Roberta's car at the hotel in New York. *She* knows me too. So, now you see :

like everyday   no matter where he was   he woke up and he's in Chicago   and everyday in Chicago is the same bright-cold   iron-clad day   no matter where he was   those first moments   Chicago

bright iron morning out that window   at the window

brilliant sun and he's blind again when he wakes up   alone again   so he'd slept thru it all   ice over the windows sent the sun in every direction   from inside   he sees brand new rivulets of blindness   the ice melts   water runs down along the glass beneath the ice   he holds his hand up against the glass half expecting to see the bones inside his fingers

ii

there's a flash   he sees the crease of his pants leg step over the
gutter onto the curb   there's the taste of sugar and rum   there's
her voice promising cake   tomorrow   there's her voice promising
tomorrow   there's the studio   mic stand coated in its ice chrome
skin   cold leather soles on a red carpet

there's a flash   he follows the angel on the stairs   *flights* in her
breath

iii

the window's a winter lake   unlocked   night is day   go
ahead   you try and tell him   go ahead and blame me

he pushes the door open and something takes a deep breath   sheets
of light break and fall to the ground   slow motion   the sharp world
of a million silver blues   silvers of sky and blue lake and silvers of sky
and blue lake   between the sky and the lake   a flash as the sheets of
light break and fall   plates of ice into an iron of blue

behind him : an empty seat   the taste of sugar and crumbs of rum on
her lip   behind him   an empty car

iv

it's over the song's over   he also knows he made this and he knows
he never had a single choice in it   he doesn't know how   he looks at
the empty seat behind him   in front of him : the pile of broken light
and the cracks in the ice spread over the window   he can see the ice
has a million decisions to make   he can see he — he can see the lake
broken open —

has no choices   never did   no one does and bright sun blares
cold on his face   steam he knows it's a memory when he feels the
warmth   a hand print on his back

he knows it's memory when he throws his shirt and coat on the sheets
of light broken under the car door swung open   that knife-crease
stepping over the gutter

the window's a broken lake

v

nude   he's on fire   he climbs over the rocks on the breakwater and
opens the blue with his body

he knows it's a memory when he feels the cool water wash hot dirt
and sand from his skin   a brown body dives under him   a trail of
air under him and down

to the bottom after a penny   sun spins off copper spins thru the
water   the water over his arms like the memory of wind light and
slow as sunshine in syrup

an August wind thru the car window   up his sleeve
a memory when he sees boys in a contest : who can hold their
breath for a minute?   exactly a minute   a contest for the body's
memory : who has practiced   off by themselves

who has waited for the third lurch   the break in the lungs

vi

a memory of a boy who'd read about the duration   before
paralysis   of a body's motion in winter water   and choices
a memory when he dives away from the heat at the surface into the
cool   away from the body in the air   the pull of the pressure   away
into darkened depth of pressure and green sound along the rippled
sand   eyes burn themselves open in freezing water

a window of decisions   the underside of the ice   rivulets of
blindness hang in the air

the penny below bursts into flame and silver disappears into blue
and there's a boy who'd know that a whale blows out one lungful
of air before a descent   otherwise   oxygen's spent pulling itself
under   quick-flash and the slow motion blink of a lover's eye in a
wonder :   an eye down the slope of a breast in a wonder

if that car's still empty?   if it's ever been empty?   or was it always
empty?   will it stay empty   can he freeze it shut   burn it black : are
these choices?

    " — when I woke this morning..."

viii

wonders if it's all the same memory   the blue and the penny and the
flame   the wide open waiting of the water   memory always hidden
from itself   again and again   the one that feels like a window in the
body   the memory's the one that hasn't ever happened before   one
that tastes sugar and rum   the low taste of rum

    her voice : *I get up in the morning, feeling that forever —*

wind in an empty pocket   flounce-rhythm of the wind   of the
one

where he thinks it's him   who turns over and over in waves of lost
silvers   waves of windows   the one who can't feel himself or the
blue   who sees a brown hand open its palm   it holds a burning
penny in its palm and lets it fall   a single copper flame that spins
as it falls   the one

who has chosen somehow   already   to know what he's decided

to do

Breaking News : *Washington Post*, January 15,
1979 : Song Writer, Singer, Falls to Death in NY

"the door to the room was locked and there was no
evidence of foul play . . . He was nominated for a second
Grammy in 1978. Winners have yet to be announced."

opens the blue   body

Acknowledgments

Grateful thanks to people who read pieces of this book as it surfaced in various guises: Michelle Chilcoat, Judith Ortiz Cofer, Joy Harjo, Terrance Hayes, Major Jackson, Sabrina Orah Mark, Dave Marsh, Harry Marten, Reginald McKnight, Leah Mirakhor, Adrienne Rich, Binyavanga Wainaina, and Craig Werner. Thanks out loud to Tayari Jones. Thanks to all associated with the Creative Writing Program at the University of Georgia. Thanks to Jordana Rich. Thanks to everyone at the University of Georgia Press, especially Nicole Mitchell, Andrew Berzanskis, Courtney Denney, Regan Huff, Anne Boston, John McLeod, and Marlene Allen. Thanks to my whole changed family. Special thanks to Julia Maher and Hilary Magee, who helped me track down scraps of information (from newspaper articles to grade-school transcripts) about Donny Hathaway. Thanks to Yusef Lateef for talking with me about his memories of Hathaway in the studio and in his classroom. Thanks to Ntone Edjabe for printing "Listening Notes : Mercy Medical Psychiatric : January 13, 1973 : Chicago, IL" in *Chimurenga*, July 2007.

Information about Donny Hathaway, while not collected in any one source, is available. Thanks to the authors of album liner notes, especially A. Scott Galloway, Ric Powell, David Nathan, Nikki Giovanni, and Roberta Flack, and to Donny Hathaway himself for the written commentary he did on his own albums. Also thanks to Eulalah Hathaway, Lalah Hathaway, Edward Howard, Leroy Hutson, Eric Mercury, Arif Mardin, Joel Dorn, Phil Upchurch, Cornell Dupree, Leon Ware, and Tina Harris for passing memories of and observations about Donny Hathaway to interviewers along the way. Special thanks to Rhino Records for keeping Hathaway's catalog of music available (*Donny Hathaway: Live*; *Donny Hathaway*; *Donny Hathaway: In Performance*; *Donny Hathaway: These Songs for You, Live!*; *Donny Hathaway: Everything Is Everything*; *Donny Hathaway: Extensions of a Man*).

And to: Richard Harrington for "Pop-Soul Vocalist Donny Hathaway at the Last Hurrah," *Washington Post*, November 25, 1977; Susan L. Taylor for "An Intimate Talk with Roberta," *Essence*, February 1989; Chris Wells for "Pop: His Soul Goes Groovin' On," *Independent* (London), February 26, 1999; D. Michael Cheers for "The Mysterious Death of Donny Hathaway," *Ebony*, April 1979; B. Comas for "Roberta and Donny Tear Up L.A.," *Soul*, June 19, 1972; Donald Anderson for "The Two Sides of Roberta Flack," *Jet*, November 29, 1979; Leida Snow for "Inevitably Roberta Flack," *High Fidelity*, May 1978; Andrew Scott for "Everything Is Everything: Donny Hathaway," *Wax Poetics* 4 (2003); Jean Williams for "Hathaway's Fund Starts Promisingly," *Billboard*, September 29, 1979; George Goodman Jr. for "Donny Hathaway, 33, Pop and Blues Singer, Dead in Hotel Plunge," *New York Times*, January 15, 1979; Pablo "Yoruba" Guzman for "Donny Hathaway, 1945–1979," *Village Voice*, February 1979; Richard Williams for "Donny — One of the New Breed," *Melody Maker*, August 7, 1971; Rick Stoff for "Donny Hathaway: 'Bright Light Burnt Out Too Soon,'" *St. Louis Globe Democrat*, January 22, 1979; Sharon C. Williams for "Wonder, Flack to Appear: Jackson to Eulogize Hathaway," *St. Louis Argus*, January 18, 1979; to Adrian Tan for the reading of Beethoven's 8th in *Inkpot.com*; George E. Curry for "He Never Forgot His Ghetto Roots," *St. Louis Post-Dispatch*, January 30, 1979; Steven Huey for his "AMG Biography"; and Jacqueline Trescott for "Donny Hathaway's Struggle with Success," *Washington Post*, January 19, 1979. Also thanks to the anonymous authors of reviews and obituaries in *Washington Post, Rolling Stone, St. Louis Sentinel, Jet, Billboard, Jazz Hot, Melody Maker, Jazz Forum*, and *Creem*.

Additional sources of information that washes through this book include: Roger Nichols, ed., *Debussy Remembered* (Faber and Faber, 1992); Robert Orledge, ed., *Satie Remembered* (Faber and Faber, 1995); James Lord, *Giacometti: A Life* (Farrar, Straus, Giroux, 1982); John Rewald, ed., *Paul Cézanne, Letters* (De Capo, 1976); Han Swafford, *The Vintage Guide to Classical Music* (Vintage, 1992); Maurice Berger, Emily Braun, Tamar Garb, Griselda Pollack, and Mason Klein, eds., *Modigliani: Beyond the Myth* (The Jewish Museum, 2004); Samuel Beckett, "Play," in *Collected Shorter Plays of Samuel Beckett* (Grove Press, 1984); *Ironwood: George Oppen: A Special Issue*, 1985; *George Oppen: Collected Poems* (New Directions, 1976).

"Under the Supervision of Schoenberg" by Alain Poirier and "Early Works by Berg" by Ulrich Kramer appear as liner notes in *Alban Berg Anton Webern: Arditti String Quartet*, Naïve Records, 1994.

A NOTE ON FICTIONAL TRUTH

Much of this book is a kind of dance between what I needed to know and not know about Donny Hathaway in order to find what I had to say. I allowed information from sources other than the music in bit by bit and usually found almost no need to adjust what I'd already written. The basic truth of this book is what I've made from the sound of Hathaway's voice, the rhythm of his work. Here and there, lyrics (both his and those written by others) appear. Quotes between sections are accurately reproduced according to sources listed above. Attributed quotations within sections of the book are likewise accurate. Passages written in Hathaway's own voice are, as far as can be known, my own transcriptions of nonverbal elements of his music.

The truths of Mr. Soul's presence in the book are lifted from the sound of John Wright's trio album about Chicago, *South Side Soul*, 1960.

In the end, beyond the scant information available in the sources above, all correspondence between the truths of this book and documented (or as-yet documented) lives of real people are a kind of unintended exhaust produced via my encounter with the tone of Hathaway's voice and the power of his music.